teenscape

A Personal Safety Programme For Teenagers

MICHELE ELLIOTT

Health
Education
Authority

Published in 1990

Health Education Authority
Hamilton House
Mabledon Place
London WC1H 9TX

ISBN 1 85448 069 3

Printed and bound in Great Britain by
Biddles Ltd, Guildford and King's Lynn

Contents

Resources

Acknowledgements

Writing and researching *Teenscape* has taken years of work. I am particularly grateful for the inspiration and support from:

Miggie Hillson, Jane Hood and Kate Hill, The Gray Coat Hospital School
Lyle Riggs, TASIS School
Sally Young, ACS School
Arnold Phillips, Teacher
Marion Lowe, Teacher
Dr Jane Wynne, Consultant Paediatrician
John Walsh, Founder Adam Walsh Foundation
Valerie Besag, Educational Psychologist
Sandra Bourne, Health Education Authority
Dave Hughes, Metropolitan Police
Dave Williams, Kent Police
Gill Robinson, Senior Advisory Teacher
John Ruddick, County Welfare Officer
To the following students for their valuable contributions:
Nicholas Hargreaves, for his excellent diary of a bully and a victim
Stephen Seymour and Jess McClellan, for their brilliant role-playing of the What If? questions
Aysha Singh for her insightful comments

Thanks to Tony Wood for his excellent illustrations

I am grateful, as well, to John Hadjipateras for his support over many years, which has made it possible for hundreds of children to be kept safe.

I should like to thank Hodder & Stoughton publishers for their kind permission to reproduce several pages from my book, *Keeping Safe: A Practical Guide to Talking with Children*, 1988 edition.

We are also very grateful to: Kingfisher Ltd; Goldman Sachs; Merrill Lynch: Conoco UK; and St Katharine by the Tower for their invaluable contributions to Kidscape.

The final word of gratitude must go to the person most responsible for the successful completion of *Teenscape* (including Tipp-Ex in taxis) – Annabel Giles, Administrator of Kidscape.

Unit 1 | User's Guide

Introduction

Welcome to *Teenscape*

This manual provides a comprehensive approach to teaching 'Good Sense Defence'. This concept teaches teenagers positive and practical ways for dealing with potentially dangerous situations.

Who is the Manual For?

Although written with teachers in mind, the manual can easily be used by other professionals working within the secondary education system. This could include health workers, police officers, educational welfare officers, educational psychologists. In short, this manual is for anyone in a position to initiate and implement the teaching of 'Good Sense Defence' to teenagers.

We hope that this manual will enable you to develop a programme for teaching 'Good Sense Defence' to teenagers, and ensure that as many young people as possible are taught how to keep safe.

How is the Manual Used?

Having taken the initiative to buy this manual, you may be wondering what to do next!

If you are not the Headteacher, but have acquired this manual for use in a secondary school, you will need to speak to your Headteacher.

Although *Teenscape* is designed to involve a wide range of professionals who work within the secondary education system, it assumes throughout that Headteachers are co-ordinating the 'Good Sense Defence' programme. Therefore parts of the manual are addressed directly to them.

However, because keeping children and young people safe is a community responsibility, it is never presumed that the implementation of the programme is the sole responsibility of the Headteacher. It is dependent upon the involvement of parents and all relevant professionals.

**What Does the
Manual Contain?**

The manual consists of four units. Each unit deals with a
different aspect of the programme. This first unit:

- shows you how to use the manual
- tells you about *Kidscape*
- gives you background information about child abuse

Turn to the first chapter of this unit. It will give you a 'guided
tour' of the rest of the manual.

Chapter One – Using the Manual

1. Manual Contents

This chapter is divided into two sections:

1. Manual contents
2. How to use the manual

Teenscape consists of the following:

Unit 1   User's Guide
To familiarise the reader with the use of the manual and with the subject of child abuse: signs, definitions, references.

Unit 2   Planning the Programme
To establish a teaching programme and school procedures.

Unit 3   The Parents' Meeting
To plan and run meetings for parents to explain the teaching programme.

Unit 4   The Lessons
To plan and teach good sense defence to teenagers.

The manual contains the information needed for planning and implementing *Teenscape* in secondary schools. It provides:

- information about child abuse and teaching good sense defence
- guidelines for planning the programme and establishing school procedures for dealing with incidents of abuse
- advice on the preparation of the meetings, workshops and lessons involved in implementing the programme
- detailed plans for running meetings for parents and teaching the lessons
- guidelines for dealing with possible disclosure from young people and adults of their experiences of child abuse
- appendices which contain information which will be of use in establishing the programme.

2. How to Use the Manual

Teenscape describes a process. The manual takes you through all the steps necessary to carry out that process.

We repeat at the beginning of each unit that **no part of the manual should be used in isolation**. We advise that the lessons should not take place until there has been a meeting for parents. The meeting for parents is held after you have established which personnel will be involved in the teaching programme and how it is to be organised. These arrangements are made after you have become familiar with the issues involved in teaching 'Good Sense Defence'.

Having worked through this manual, unit by unit, you will have all the information you need to carry out each stage in the process of organising and implementing the programme. From our experience, we know that, if you try to take short cuts, you could create problems, perhaps for the school or for a teacher, a parent or a student.

Process

As well as providing a process, the manual is a source of valuable information for people working with teenagers in the formal education system. Ideally, every secondary school should have at least one manual. 'Good Sense Defence' is an ongoing process which, to be effective, will obviously need reinforcement in order to become an integrated part of young people's everyday lives. The manual is therefore designed to be used and re-used over many years as a basis of continuing the teaching of personal safety.

All those planning the programme in a secondary school should have an opportunity to study the whole manual prior to the programme being implemented. The programme is more effective when the knowledge and information contained in the manual is shared in advance amongst everyone involved.

Routing

At the end of each chapter, there is a set of instructions. These instructions are your 'routing guide'. They tell you where to go and what to do next.

What to do Now

If you have ten minutes:

- skim through the manual so that you have an idea of how it is laid out
- read the Introduction and Contents pages for Units 2, 3 and 4. They explain the purpose and summarise the content of each unit
- look at some of the routing instructions at the end of each chapter so that you can get a sense of how they work
- plan to spend an hour when you can look at the manual in more detail
- when you have finished, return to this point in the manual.

If you have longer:

- read Chapter Three – Background Information
- look at the lesson plans in Unit 4: The Lessons
- when you have finished, return to this point in the manual

Turn to Chapter Two of this manual: Kidscape. This explains the basis of the 'Good Sense Defence' programme.

Chapter Two – Kidscape

This chapter deals with:

- the pilot project
- the development of *Kidscape*
- *Teenscape*

It is divided into four sections:

1. Who
2. Pilot Project
3. Development of *Kidscape*
4. *Teenscape*

1. Who

Kidscape was founded by Michele Elliott, a teacher and child psychologist who has lived and worked in the UK since 1971. She has chaired Home Office and World Health Organisation committees on the prevention of child abuse. She is the author of numerous articles and books, including *Keeping Safe: A Practical Guide to Talking with Children, The Willow Street Kids: It's Your Right to be Safe* and *Feeling Happy, Feeling Safe*. She is married to a teacher and has two sons.

2. Pilot Project

The *Kidscape Primary Kit* is based on a two-year pilot project from 1984 to 1986, which involved 4,000 children, their parents and teachers. It was set up after discovering that there were no prevention programmes in Britain for schools which dealt with subjects like bullying, getting lost and how to avoid abuse. Although *Stranger Danger* was widely taught, *Kidscape* wanted to incorporate into the curriculum a greater variety of dangers faced by children.

After gathering information on programmes from several countries, visiting schools and taking part in training courses, the *Child Assault Prevention Programme* was set up as a pilot project. Contacts were made with the NSPCC, police, social workers, psychiatrists, teachers, and others working with children to explore the best way to implement the pilot project.

It soon became clear that the material and methods from other countries were not suitable for schools in Britain. Many were based upon outside agencies coming in and teaching children. Some were full of shock/horror stories. We felt the issue of safety should be low-key safety and be part of the curriculum so that children not only learned strategies for keeping safe from a variety of dangers, but that they addressed ideas of rights and responsibilities. Keeping safe from sexual abuse was only one component of the entire programme.

3. Development of Kidscape

Kidscape is based on these priorities:

- parental involvement
- teacher involvement
- multi-disciplinary approach
- existence and knowledge of the procedures to be followed in cases of abuse
- the importance of not making young people distrustful of loving relationships and normal, everyday affection
- the need for children to be given general strategies for staying safe:
  — from bullies
  — from strangers who might harm them
  — from people known to them who might try to harm them

The pilot project led to thousands of enquiries and requests for workshops in schools. The only way to meet this need was to develop a programme so that it could be implemented within schools by those working with children. The *Kidscape* programmes emphasise practical, positive ways to help keep children safe, always involving adults in the process. The *Kidscape Under-Fives* programme has the same emphasis: low-key, matter-of-fact and non-sensational.

4. Teenscape

Teenscape was developed from the pilot project and from Michele's previous work with teenagers from 1968 to 1984. This manual is a comprehensive approach to teaching 12–16 year olds 'Good Sense Defence'. The manual makes it possible for parents, teachers and other concerned adults to teach young people, in a non-frightening, practical way to keep themselves safe. It involves adults so that young people are not left unsupported with the total responsibility for keeping themselves safe.

Although written for teachers, the manual can easily be used by other professionals working within the secondary education system.

Teenscape lessons discuss issues such as:

- Trusting intuition
- Saying no
- Bullying
- Crime
- Rights and responsibilities
- Abuse
- Relationships
- Getting help
- Common sense self defence
- Addiction
- Gambling

It provides an introduction from which teachers can do more in-depth work.

Chapter Three – Background Information

This chapter deals with:

- definitions of child sexual abuse
- the reported scale of the problem
- the known characteristics of offenders
- why young people should be taught prevention techniques
- recognising possible signs of sexual abuse
- dealing with disclosures of sexual abuse

It is divided into five sections:

1. Child sexual abuse
2. The scale of the problem
3. Teaching prevention
4. What you can do
5. Recognising signs

1. Child Sexual Abuse

The *Kidscape* programmes deal with the whole range of good sense defence which involves keeping all children safe. Most concerns expressed by young people, such as bullying, are fairly well known to adults who work with them. Unfortunately, most adults who work with young people have never been given any information about what to do if a young person is approached in a sexually inappropriate way by someone known to them. Even though the lessons incorporate many other issues, the teachers in the pilot project expressed a need to have background information about child abuse and in particular about child sexual abuse. Because of these requests, this unit presents background information for adults so they will feel more confident in dealing with this emotive subject.

Definitions

Children are naturally affectionate and seek the attention of adults. When any significantly older person uses a child as a sexual object or partner, it is inappropriate and irresponsible behaviour. (1)

There is no totally satisfactory definition of child sexual abuse. Many committees and government agencies have tried to define exactly this type of abuse, but it seems impossible to find one definition on which everyone agrees. The definitions given below are a helpful starting point: (in Britain, a child refers to anyone under the age of sixteen).

Kempe's definition is widely accepted:

'Sexual abuse is defined as the involvement of dependent developmentally immature children and adolescents in sexual activities they do not truly comprehend, to which they are unable to give informed consent, or that violate the social taboos of family roles'. (2)

The definition used in the 1984 MORI survey by Baker and Duncan stated that:

'A child is sexually abused when another person, who is sexually mature, involves a child in any activity which the other person expects to lead to their sexual arousal. This might involve intercourse, touching, exposure of the sexual organs, showing pornographic material or talking about sexual things in an erotic way.' (3)

2. The Scale of the Problem

The definitions of sexual abuse cover a wide range of abuse from 'flashers' and obscene telephone calls to rape and incest. It is important to note that the statistics are usually based upon this entire range of offences. In reading the following statistics, also note that they are based upon *reported* incidents from which estimates have been made. A 'sexually abusive experience' does not necessarily mean rape or incest.

In Britain

In 1984, a questionnaire was devised by Baker and Duncan as part of a MORI survey in Great Britain.

From this survey, it has been estimated that approximately 4.5 million British adults alive today had sexually abusive experiences as children. Based upon these same figures, some experts have estimated that as many as 1,117,000 of the children alive in Britain today could have at least one sexually abusive experience by the time they are 15 years old; 143,000 of those could involve abuse within the family. (3)

The questionnaire was administered as part of the MORI survey to a representative sample of 2019 men and women:

- 13% did not answer this part of the survey
- 10% who answered this part of the survey reported being sexually abused before the age of 16.

Of this 10%

- 12% of the women reported sexually abusive experiences
- 8% of men reported the same
- 14% reported abuse was within the family
- 51% reported abusive situations involving no physical contact
- 44% involved physical contact, but not sexual intercourse
- 5% reported sexual intercourse
- 63% reported a single abusive experience
- 23% reported being abused repeatedly by the same person
- 14% reported multiple abuse by a number of people.

In 1988, MORI conducted a survey for the London Programme with 664 young people in the south-east between the ages of 16–24. The results were shown on the London Programme on 13 October 1988:

- 8% (1 in 12) had a sexual experience before the age of 16 with an adult
- 17% of the abusers were within the child's family
- 74% of the abusers were outside the child's family
- 9% of the children were abused by adults from both inside and outside the family
- 45% of the children were aged 14–15 at the time of the first incident
- 55% of the children were under the age of 13 at the time of the first incident
- 33% of the children told someone what happened
- 66% did not tell anyone what happened

In a survey on sexual abuse in 1982 devised by Baker for *19* magazine, 36% of the girls who responded reported that they had been sexually abused as children. Althouh self-selecting, the 3000 questionnaires returned by readers gave valuable information in understanding the problem:

- there was no social class difference in the incidence of child sexual abuse
- the ages of the offenders ranged from 14 to 70
- 98% of the reported offenders were male
- 90% of the offenders were known to the child – many were family members
- 85% said that the abuse ended because someone else found out or because they said no
- in 10% of cases, the abuse stopped only when the victim ran away or attempted suicide

Many of the respondents to the *19* magazine survey reported problems in later life related to the abuse, such as negative self-images, difficulties in forming relationships and in dealing with stress. This was particularly true for victims of incest. (4)

The registers managed by the NSPCC showed a dramatic increase in the number of reported cases of all types of abuse of children from 1983 to 1987. The number of children registered more than doubled from 1115 to 2307. (5)

Donald West of the Institute of Criminology of Cambridge University reported that 46% of the women in his survey had been sexually abused as children. This was based on the responses of 600 women, half of whom had never told anyone of their expriences. One third said they still suffered some effects from the abuse. (6)

In a survey of women in London, Ruth Hall found that 21% of the 1236 respondents remembered being sexually abused as children. One third said it had happened more than once. (7)

Outside Britain

Those countries which investigate and report openly about their social problems show similar statistics on child sexual abuse to those provided by the MORI survey. Some studies in these countries indicate a higher estimate based on reported incidents. The US Department of Health and Human Services report that up to 500,000 children are sexually abused each year. (8) In West Germany the police annually receive 20,000 reports of sexual offences against children. (9)

In one US study by David Finkelhor, it was found that:

- 19% of women reported sexual victimisation as children
- 9% of men reported the same

From this, Finkelhor estimates that between 2 million and 5 million women have been sexually abused as children. (10) (In the US a child is anyone under the age of 18).

It is estimated that 1 in 7 boys in the US has had a sexually abusive experience. (11)

In another US study by Landis, questionnaires were sent to 1800 university students. 33% of those who responded reported being sexually abused as children. (12)

Diana Russell, in a US study of sexual abuse involving women, found that 38% of those involved reported having had a sexually abusive experience before the age of 18. (13)

Going back to the 1950s, the Kinsey Survey revealed that 1:4 of 4400 women surveyed had been sexually abused before the age of 18.

There are many statistical surveys beginning to emerge from European countries. A recent study in Norway shows that 14% of the men and 18% of the women reported having been sexually abused as children.

These figures are presented to give an overview of the problem and not to focus unduly on the statistics themselves. What is becoming increasingly apparent is that asking people about their experiences as children has produced, and will continue to uncover, evidence which will add to the statistics.

Collecting information or evidence from people about sexually abusive experiences in their childhood does not increase the problem. Because people are finally being given permission to tell, the conspiracy of silence is now being broken. For them the problem was already there; it has not been suddenly created.

The true extent of the problem of child sexual abuse is still unknown. Because surveys are aimed at today's adults, it is still not possible to gain a real picture of what is currently happening to today's children.

Who are the
Offenders?

There is no satisfactory answer to this question. Using Nicolas Groth's definitions may help to explain that people who abuse children do so for different reasons. He places them in two basic categories:

- **The Fixated Child Molester**
  This type of offender has a compulsive sexual attraction to children. From his adolescence onwards, children have been the primary or sole object of sexual interest. Any sexual involvement with people of his own age is of a temporary nature and never replaces his preference for children. In general a fixated molester often appears to identify with children and may wish to remain one himself. Thus, the victims are often boys, used in a narcissistic sense rather than as a homosexual object.

- **The Regressed Child Molester**
  This type of offender's sexual involvement with children is usually a temporary (though it sometimes becomes permanent) departure from usual sexual relationships with an adult. Often there has been no previous sexual interest in children, but the stresses of the adult world lead him to refer to children as sexual objects. He has grown up, but cannot cope with adult life, especially in his relationships with his partner. This sexual interest in children may come and go as the times of stress in his life change.
  Since regressed child molesters use children as a substitute for adult relationships and many are married or living with women, the substitute child is usually a girl. They feel more confident with her than with a woman their own age.

According to Groth, offenders are often immature, manipulative, feel inadequate as people and tend to blame others for their own failings. Many were victims of abuse as children. In one of Nicolas Groth's prison studies of child molesters, it was found that 80% of the offenders had been themselves either physically or sexually abused as children. (14) Therefore, it can be said that they, too, are the victims of child abuse.

In 97% of the *reported* cases of child sexual abuse in Britain the abusers were men. (15) This does not mean that the vast majority of men are abusers. Much less is known at this time about the fewer reported cases involving women abusers. The trauma of the abuse to the victim is as great regardless of the gender of the abuser.

In one US study of sexual offenders, it was found that, on average, each offender had:

- attempted 238 child molestations
- completed 166 molestations
- created 75 child victims

In the same study when the offenders described their first offence against a child:

- 84% said it was a hands-on experience such as fondling
- 13% said they had exposed themselves
- 3% began by voyeurism or fetishes

It was also found that approximately 30% of the child molesters reported that alcohol increased their sexual arousal.

Many of the sex offenders in this study (42%) had deviant fantasies at a young age, some as early as 12 or 13 years old. A way must be found to identify and treat such young people before their behaviour becomes harmful to others. (16)

The various studies of offenders seem to show that they do not 'stand out'. Many appear to be normal people leading normal lives. They come from every background, race and social class. Many are married with children of their own. People are usually quite surprised if they find out that someone they know has sexually abused a child. It is difficult to reconcile that anyone who looks and acts normally could be a child molester. Often, therefore, when a child reports an incident of abuse, many adults prefer to think that the child is lying or has manipulated the adult.

Who is Responsible?

Legally the adult is always responsible for sexual offences against children. See Appendix 1 for definitions of criminal offences.

Do Children/Teenagers Make it up?

It is rare for young people to make false accusations about sexual abuse. For more details see Unit 3: Appendix 1, Common Adult Concerns.

Cycles of Abuse

Surveys have shown that many offenders have themselves suffered sexual or physical abuse as children. The re-enactment of that abuse on a new generation of children often gives them a sense of power and may be the only way they have learned to interact. It is this cycle that must be broken into in order to keep children safe.

This is not to say that all sexually abused children will become offenders as adults. Most children who have been abused grow up to be caring adults and parents.

In Summary

Even given all the studies and statistics currently available, it is not easy to get an accurate picture of the extent of the problem. The difficulty in obtaining information about the incidents of child sexual abuse is only now beginning to be overcome. As concern grows and people are more willing to believe, those who have been abused are becoming more confident in speaking about the damaging secrets of their childhood.

The literature also indicates that the effects of child sexual abuse can be measured by a range of social indicators: addictive alcoholism and drug dependency; behaviours such as suicides, delinquency and truancy. It can also lead to mental illness and emotional disorders.

As a result of the studies of offenders, it may be possible eventually to intervene at a point which prevents deviant fantasies from becoming behavioural patterns. Whilst there is no accurate estimate of the numbers of offenders, a picture is beginning to emerge of the compulsive behaviour which seems to create so many victims per offender. Further studies may lead to more effective treatments, both for victims and offenders. Treatment is only seen to be required, however, after the fact. A far better strategy is to prevent it happening in the first place.

3. Teaching Prevention

From the time they are very young, children are taught many rules about keeping safe: crossing the road; being careful near water; avoiding harmful medicines; and not playing with matches. Children are also taught about not talking to strangers. Whilst this is obviously a good idea, statistics show that at least 75% of reported cases of sexual abuse are committed by someone the child knows. So we must teach more than never to speak to strangers.

Talking to Teenagers

It is also important to realise that the vast majority of children and young people have never been and will never be sexually abused. Therefore, it is not a good idea to use fear, nor to give more information than is needed to keep safe. For example, some books and videos advocate teaching children and young people not to trust anyone. Some of these materials use explicit language and explain the term 'sexual abuse', even to five year olds.

Kidscape never uses the words 'sex' or 'abuse' when teaching young children good sense defence. Children should not be introduced to the concept of sex in connection with abuse because of the effect it could have on their emerging ideas of sexuality.

This approach also makes it easier for those children who may have already experienced sexual abuse, as the lesson does not threaten them or make them feel as if the teacher is talking about them. All children seem to know about and understand good and bad touching in a variety of situations. It is a very comfortable way for children to explore how to keep safe.

With teenagers it is possible to be more explicit. It is suggested that in the lessons to younger teenagers, the terms sex and abuse not be used unless raised by the students themselves. We have found that most teenagers have heard about child abuse and sexual abuse from the media. Therefore it is rare for a teenager to be completely unaware these days.

Teenagers enjoy talking about themselves and their experiences. *Kidscape*'s methods are based upon getting them to be actively involved in the lessons and using their experiences to make the learning relevant to them. For example, most teenagers can tell about a time that a bully accosted them. Equally, they know what kind of affection or touching they do and don't like. This is the basis of getting them to think about what to do in a variety of situations in which they may have to say no and get some kind of adult help.

In the *Kidscape* 'Good Sense Defence' Programme, teenagers are taught:

- General rules about keeping safe
- How to deal with bullies
- How to stay safe while out
- To say 'No' when someone, even someone they know, tries to touch them in a confusing, frightening or unsafe way
- To refuse to keep secrets about any kind of touching
- To always seek help
- To always talk to someone if anything happens which frightens them
- To discuss their rights and responsibilities, crime, trusting their own intuition and the reasons that people become addicted to drugs, alcohol and cigarettes.

Does Good Sense Defence Help?

Our experience has shown that talking with teenagers in a matter-of-fact way about good sense defence has been very successful. This opens up many of the concerns that they have already shared with their friends. Rather than the often inaccurate and frightening tales that they hear from their peers, good sense defence provides positive and practical ways with which they can help themselves.

Furthermore, the programme creates an invaluable, interactive process between teenagers and adults they can trust.

We have been told of numerous incidents of teenagers using good sense defence to keep safe after having had the lessons. Two brothers were accosted by a bully in the park near their home. He demanded money to let them pass. They yelled 'No' together very loudly and the bully didn't know what to do next, so startled was he that anyone younger would say no, he just walked away. Another group of youngsters were near their school when a man came up and flashed at them. They all turned away without a word. A young teenager who had been sexually abused was able to tell the school nurse. The abuse was stopped.

So prevention can work in different ways:

- Teenagers learn that they can share their concerns with a responsible adult
- Misconceptions that arise when they talk about staying safe are cleared up
- Teenagers can use good sense defence to plan ahead and avoid getting into dangerous situations
- Teenagers can seek help for something that has already happened to them
- It can allow teenagers to talk to their parents or other adults and know that they will be believed and helped
- For those being abused within the family, it provides a way to tell about what is happening and get help

4. What You Can Do

This manual provides you with a comprehensive programme to help teenagers learn good sense defence. By using this resource, you will be able to:

- set up a meeting with all those who work with young people in your school
- set up a meeting for parents to help provide them with ways to continue the learning process about good sense defence
- teach the students in one lesson, or preferably a series of lessons, how to help keep themselves safe in a variety of situations.

Young people may react differently to concepts dealt with in the lesson.

One problem is that some teenagers may feel that they have done something wrong. This could be exacerbated in more serious cases of sexual abuse or where the abuse is ongoing. It is therefore important that they are not made to feel self-conscious or in any way responsible for the experience, or for not having told about it before.

Disclosure

As talking to someone is one of the basic messages of good sense defence, it is possible that a student will tell you about something that has happened to them.

The majority of disclosures that you are likely to come across will involve flashers and obscene telephone calls or bullying incidents. These experiences can be very upsetting and talking about the experience and eliciting the help of an adult will obviously be a great relief.

There may be other disclosures of a more serious nature, such as beatings, emotional abuse or sexual abuse by someone known. (See Appendix 1 for the legal definition of incest.) These types of offences are potentially the most damaging because of the betrayal of trust. Incest is also the form of sexual abuse that is likely to continue over a prolonged period of time, thus creating the worst possible effects in the life of the young person.

To avoid any misunderstanding, we would emphasise that we are not talking about stranger assaults or incest alone. The range of child sexual abuse includes these and all the situations in between. However, in the vast majority of cases of child sexual abuse the offence will involve someone known to the teenager.

Dealing with Disclosure

In the case of disclosures about incidents such as flashers, keep a record of those that are reported by children or adults in a school log book. You can either use the suggested format we provide (see Appendix 2.2, p. 60) or devise one of your own. Make a note of:

- who saw the incident
- when it happened
- where it happened
- any information that can be remembered which might be helpful

Information like this can help police to identify patterns in behaviour, which might lead to the person being caught.

It is possible that some of the incidents that are disclosed may be more serious. It can be difficult to know what to do when this happens. You are not expected to be an expert in the field of child abuse, nor in the field of child counselling. You can, however, listen to, believe and support the student through a crisis. You might be the only person that a teenager feels able to talk to. In other sections of this manual, we suggest:

- ways in which the school can establish procedures for communicating such disclosures to a range of agencies, such as the police, social services, NSPCC (Unit 2)
- what to do if a young person discloses to you – how should you react? (Unit 4)

5. Recognising Signs

The indications are that in a class of thirty children, there is a possibility that three will have had a sexually abusive experience. Statistically, this is more likely in a class of older children (i.e. age 10 and older). *However this is only an average figure based on the MORI survey.* We have found many classes in which no child disclosed and some classes in which half the children told of incidents such as indecent exposure or being talked to in an obscene way on the telephone or at bus stops.

How Can I Tell if it is Happening?

Unless the young person tells, it is difficult sometimes to know. Recognising some of the signs, particularly of more serious, long-term abuse, such as incest or being interferred with by someone known to the teenagers, is important for all adults working with young people.

Teenagers who have been abused usually show the effects in some way. Below is a list of the signs that have been known to characterise the various forms of abuse. Although these signs do not necessarily indicate that a child has been abused, the possibility should be investigated if a student is exhibiting a number of these or any one of them to a marked degree.

Signs of Abuse

1. Signs of Physical Abuse

- unexplained injuries or burns, particularly if they are recurrent
- improbable excuses given to explain injuries
- refusal to discuss injuries
- untreated injuries
- admission of punishment which appears excessive
- fear of parents being contacted
- bald patches
- withdrawal from physical contact
- arms and legs kept covered in hot weather
- fear of returning home
- fear of medical help
- self-destructive tendencies
- aggression towards others
- chronic running away

2. Signs of Emotional Abuse

- physical, mental and emotional development lags
- admission of punishment which appears excessive
- over-reaction to mistakes
- continual self-deprecation
- sudden speech disorders
- fear of new situations
- inappropriate emotional responses to painful situations

- neurotic behaviour (e.g. rocking; hair-twisting; thumb-sucking)
- self-mutilation
- fear of parents being contacted
- extremes of passivity or aggression
- drug/solvent abuse
- chronic running away
- compulsive stealing/scavenging

3. Signs of Neglect

- constant hunger
- poor personal hygiene
- constant tiredness
- poor state of clothing
- emaciation
- frequent lateness or non-attendance at school
- untreated medical problems
- destructive tendencies
- low self-esteem
- neurotic behaviour (see 2)
- no social relationships
- chronic running away
- compulsive stealing or scavenging

(The following is an excerpt from *Keeping Safe: A Practical Guide to Talking with Children*[1])

4. Signs of Sexual Abuse

Young people from the age of 12 may:
- be chronically depressed/suicidal
- use drugs/drink excessively/self-mutilate
- have unexplained pregnancies
- be anorexic/bulimic
- run away chronically
- be inappropriately seductive
- be fearful about certain people like relatives and friends
- not be allowed to go out on dates or have friends around
- have soreness, bleeding in the genital or anal areas or in the throat
- find excuses not to go home or to a particular place
- have recurring nightmares/be afraid of the dark
- be unable to concentrate/play truant
- exhibit a sudden change in school/work habits
- have a 'friend who has a problem' and then tell about the abuse of the friend
- have chronic ailments such as stomach and headaches
- sexually abuse a child, sibling or friend
- be withdrawn, isolated/become excessively worried
- have outbursts of anger or irritability
- be fearful of undressing for gym
- have unexplained sums of money

Fifteen-year-old Karen had been sexually abused for years by her stepfather. He told her she was his 'special girl', bought her presents and gave her large sums of money. She had the major responsibilities in the house and was never allowed to go out with friends, girls or boys. She was told that if she disclosed the abuse to anyone, the family would fall apart and she would be the cause.

Because the abuse had been long-term, she did not show sudden changes in behaviour, but had exhibited several signs through the years. She had attempted suicide on two occasions, had become anorexic, could not concentrate in school, was often depressed and continually had health problems.

Karen's plight should have been uncovered years previously, given the number of alarming signals. The abuse was only stopped because an alert gym teacher recognised that Karen's symptoms could be indicative of sexual abuse.

Unfortunately, Karen's stepfather did not admit to the abuse and her mother turned against her. Although Karen disclosed the abuse, she later retracted. Karen went to live with her grandmother, but she still needs long-term therapy to come to terms with what has happened. Perhaps the outcome would have been better had the abuse been recognised earlier, but we will never know.

The different kinds of abuse can also be interrelated: a sexually abused teenager will be emotionally abused and perhaps neglected or physically abused as well. Almost by definition any young person who has been physically or sexually abused or neglected has also been emotionally abused.

Some of the characteristic signs of abuse are the same, so there will be duplications in the lists provided.

It is important to note that these lists are possible indicators of abuse. *Many of the signs could have other explanations.*

One teacher concluded that most of her class exhibited one sign or another – the lists are useful as a reference, but beware of over-reacting.

This chapter has been designed to provide all of the background information you might need in implementing the programme. Should you wish to find out more, Appendix 2 provides some selected materials which may be helpful. The books listed give interested individuals further information about child abuse. Videos are also reviewed.

Now turn to Unit 2: Planning the Programme and read the first chapter in the unit. This explains what steps need to be taken to start planning a teaching programme.

References

1. Elliott, M. *Keeping Safe: A Practical Guide to Talking with Children*, Hodder & Stoughton, 1988.
2. Kempe, R.S. and Kempe, C.H. *Child Abuse*, Fontana/Open Books, 1978.
3. Baker, A and Duncan, S. 'Child Sexual Abuse: A study of Prevalence in Great Britain' in *Child Abuse & Neglect* Vol. 9, 1985.
4. Newman, L. 'Sexual Abuse within the Family' in *19* magazine, May 1983.
5. Creighton, S.J. and Noyes, P. *Child Abuse Trends in England and Wales 1983–1987*, from the National Society for the Prevention of Cruelty to Children, July 1989.
6. West, D. *Sexual Victimisation*, Gower Publishing Co. Ltd, 1985.
7. Hall, R. *Ask Any Woman: A London inquiry into rape and sexual assault*, Falling Wall Press, 1985.
8. *Child Sexual Abuse: Incest, Assault and Sexual Exploitation*, from the US Department of Health and Human Services, 1982.
9. Smolowe, J., Clifton, T. and Echikson, W. 'A Hidden Epidemic' in *Newsweek International*, May 4, 1984.
10. Finkelhor, D. *Sexually Victimized Children*, Free Press, 1979.
11. Swift, C. 'Sexual Victimization of Children: An Urban Mental Health Centre Survey' in *Victimology* 2, 1977.
12. Landis, J. *Father–Daughter Incest*, Harvard University Press, 1981.
13. Russell, Diana, 'Incidence and prevalence of intrafamilial and extrafamilial sexual abuse of female children,' *Child Abuse & Neglect*, Vol 7, 1983, pp. 133–146.
14. Groth, N., Hobson, W. and Gray, T. 'The Child Molester: Clinical Observations' in *Social Work & Child Sexual Abuse*, 1982.
15. Mrazek, P.B., Lynch, M. and Bentovim, A. 'Recognition of Child Sexual Abuse in the United Kingdom' in Mrazek, P.B. and Kempe, C.H. (eds.) *Sexually Abused Children and Their Families*, Pergamon Press, 1981.
16. Abel, G., Mittelman, M. and Beczer, J. *Sexual Offenders: Results of Assessment and Recommendations for Treatment*, New York State Psychiatric Institute and the Department of Psychiatry, College of Physicians and Surgeons, Columbia University, New York City.

**Appendix 1.1 –
Criminal Offences**

Rape

Forceable sexual intercourse. Consent by a child to intercourse is immaterial. It is not necessary for intercourse to be completed. Penetration to any degree is sufficient.
(Section 1(1) Sexual Offences Act 1956 as amended by Sexual Offences (Amendment) Act 1976).

Unlawful Sexual Intercourse

It is an offence for a man to have intercourse with a girl under 16 to whom he is not married. It is not necessary for intercourse to be completed. Penetration to any degree is sufficient. It is a defence in respect of girls aged 14–16 where:
(i) There is a marriage which is invalid under English law.
(ii) The man is under 24, has not previously been charged with a similar offence and reasonably believes the girl to be over 16.
(Sections 5 and 6 Sexual Offences Act 1956)

Incest

Sexual intercourse between persons related within certain degrees.
Consent is immaterial:
    By a woman over 16 to have intercourse with a man she knows to be her father, grandfather, son, brother (or half-brother). By a man to have intercourse with a woman he knows to be his daughter, grand-daughter, mother or sister (including half-sister).
(Sections 10 and 11 Sexual Offences Act 1956)

It is an offence for a man to incite a girl under 16 to have incestuous sexual intercourse with him.
(Section 54 Criminal Law Act 1977)

Buggery

Unlawful sexual intercourse by penetration of the anus. Penetration to any degree is sufficient.
(Section 12 Sexual Offences Act 1956 as amended by Sexual Offences Act 1967)

Assault with Intent to Commit Buggery

An alternative offence where the act falls short of buggery, or penetration cannot be proved.
(Section 16 Sexual Offences Act 1956)

Gross Indecency

Refers to acts of indecency only between males. Physical contact
is not always necessary. Examples of gross indecency are: mutual
masturbation, oral-genital contact. Offences include committing
an act of gross indecency, being party to the commission, or
procuring the commission of the act. The word 'gross' has no
significance in law.
(Section 13 Sexual Offences Act 1956 as amended by Sexual
Offences Act 1967)

Indecent Assault

No formal legal definition but there must be an assault: that is
an application of force or hostile act or gesture, and it must be
accompanied by circumstances of indecency. It does not matter
how minor the assault is if it occurs in circumstances of
indecency. Examples of indecent assault are: touching a child
whilst suggesting an indecent act, touching the inside of a child's
thigh.
(Sections 14 and 15 Sexual Offences Act 1956)

Indecent Conduct With or Towards a Child

This can be done by any person who commits an act of
indecency with or towards a child under 14 or who incites a child
under 14 to commit such an act. Examples of this are: adults
who ask children to touch them or an adult who asks two
children to commit an indecent act on each other (providing one
child is under 14).
(Section 1 Indecency with Children Act 1960)

*Causing or Encouraging Prostitution or Intercourse with or
Indecent Assault on a Girl under 16*

Person committing the offence will be the person having
responsibility for the girl. It is sufficient to allow the girl to
consort with or enter into, or continue in the employment of a
prostitute or person of known immoral character. The implication
is that the person must have knowledge of or allow the action to
continue.
(Sections 25, 26 and 28 Sexual Offences Act 1956)

Indecent Photographs of Children

It is an offence for a person to:
(a)   Take or allow indecent photographs of a child to be taken
OR

(b) distribute or show any such photographs OR
(c) have in their possession indecent photographs with a view to their distribution or publication.

NOTE: 'Children' means persons under 16
'Indecent' is not defined but will be a matter for the Court
'Indecent photographs' includes films and copies of films and photographs. It also includes negatives and any form of video recording. A single frame of any film is sufficient.

In cases of unidentified children in indecent photographs, the age may be determined by the Court.

Any photograph which portrays a child in an indecent scene, even though the child may not be pictured indecently, is covered by the Act.
(Section 1 Protection of Children Act 1978).

Appendix 1.2 – Books

Besag, V. *Bullies and Their Victims in Schools: A Guide to Understanding and Management*, Open University Press, 1989. The first half of this excellent book is an in-depth review of the research into relationships, bullies, victims, families, and the social behaviour of children. The second half is a practical guide on how to deal with the problem.

Creighton, S.J. and Noyes, P. *Child Abuse Trends in England and Wales 1983–1987*, NSPCC, 1989.
Gives the current statistics and trends that are being uncovered in the area of child abuse. It is the largest, continuous study of child abuse in Britain.

Department of Education and Science, Circular No. 4/88, July 1988.
'Working Together for the Protection of Children from Abuse: Procedures within the Education Service'. Gives guidelines to LEAs, teachers and staff about how to protect children from abuse.

Department of Health and Social Security, Circular 26/88, July 1988.
'Working Together for the Protection of Children from Abuse'. This circular introduces a guide consolidating and updating existing guidance on inter-agency work in the field of child abuse.

Elliott, M. *Keeping Safe: A Practical Guide to Talking with Children*, Hodder & Stoughton, 1988.
Easily understood, step-by-step guide to talking about keeping safe from a variety of dangers from bullying, to sexual abuse, to drugs, AIDS, gambling, travelling by public transport, etc.

Elliott, M. *The Willow Street Kids*, Andre Deutsch (hardcover)/ Pan (paperback), 1986.
Based upon true stories of children, this book has been written in an entertaining way to help children figure out what to do in a variety of situations, from bullying to getting lost, to unwelcome advances from adults, known and unknown. Written for 7 to 11 year olds, it can be used with teenagers with lower reading levels.

Finklehor, D. *Child Sexual Abuse, New Theory and Research*, Collier Macmillan, 1984.
Comprehensive book which includes discussion about why there are more male abusers; boys as victims; the most current research on child sexual abuse.

Hall, R.E. *Ask Any Woman: A London inquiry into rape and sexual assault*, Falling Wall Press, 1985.
Based upon a self-selecting survey of women in London, it relates their experiences of being raped and of being victims of child sexual abuse.

Kempe, R.S. and Kempe, C.H. *Child Abuse*, Fontana/Open Books, 1978.
Clearly written and comprehensive guide to understanding child abuse.

Kempe, R.S. and Kempe, C.H. *The Common Secret: Sexual Abuse of Children and Adolescents*, W.H. Freeman and Company, 1984.
Practical, comprehensive resource which takes an insightful look into child sexual abuse.

Lynch, M. and Roberts, J. *Consequences of Child Abuse*, Academic Press, 1982.
A complete overview to the consequences of what happens in cases of child abuse, including legal and medical implications.

Moore, J. *The ABC of Child Abuse Work*, Gower, 1985.
Practical guide with suggestions for helping abusive families.

Morris, M. *If I Should Die before I Wake*, Dell, 1982.
Powerful, fictionalised story of a victim of father–daughter incest.

Mrazek, P.B. and Kempe, C.H. (eds). *Sexually Abused Children and their Families*, Pergamon Press, 1981.
An anthology by experts in the fields of child sexual abuse.

NSPCC 'Developing a Child Centred Response to Sexual Abuse', 1984.
A working party report on child sexual abuse listing signs of possible sexual abuse, particularly within the family.

Porter, R. (ed). *Child Sexual Abuse within the Family*, Tavistock Publications, 1984.
Provides guidance on the actions to be taken by professionals involved in the management of cases of sexual abuse within the family.

Renvoize, J. *Incest – A Family Pattern*, Routledge & Kegan Paul, 1982.
Well-researched, easily-read book which gives information on current methods of treatment in the US and Britain.

Rudinger, E. 'Children, Parents and the Law', Consumers' Association, *Which?* 1986.
A clear, concise guide to the law, also listing sources of advice, voluntary organisations and support groups.

Videos

There has been a recent flood of 'prevention' videos into Britain, the vast majority of which have come from Canada and the U.S. The videos are intended to make children confident to deal with the possibility that someone might try to touch them in an inappropriate way.

Because the subject of child sexual abuse is in high profile now, many adults may be tempted to buy a video, put young people in front of it and hope that they get the message.

There are several problems with this approach:

- Teenagers should be introduced to the ideas of keeping safe in an interactive relationship with a responsible adult. This method does not include this.
- Videos do not provide sufficient flexibility to deal sensitively with this subject with groups.
- Most of the videos do not emphasise good hugs and kisses and positive relationships with adults enough. Young people could get the message that 'it is best not to trust people'.
- Adults usually have had no preparation for the questions that teenagers will ask.
- Young people will have questions and the discussion should be continuous. This is not possible with a video presentation. This can easily lead to misunderstanding about what the outcome message is on the part of the teenagers.
- Adults think that young people understand what to do because they have seen the video, and these young people may therefore be left more vulnerable because they have not understood.
- If a teenager does understand and has something to tell, the adults will not have been prepared to deal with the disclosure.
- Some videos are too long, too gimmicky and too confusing.

There is no substitute for talking with children and young people, particularly in an area as important as personal safety. When teenagers, parents and teachers have been through a comprehensive programme and are familiar with all the issues, some videos might prove useful as part of a follow-up lesson. The adult showing the video will then know how to deal with questions; parents will have had meetings and many will have already approached the subject with their children because of the lessons and the material sent home. Once this process has been set up, a video could be used as a tool, but not as the primary means to help keep young people safe.

Unit 2

Planning the Programme and Establishing School Procedures

Introduction

This Unit explains how to:

- develop a programme for teaching good sense defence in secondary schools
- establish procedures for dealing with possible incidents of disclosure of child abuse

The basis of the programme was developed over a two-year period in schools throughout the UK. During that time it was found to be essential that schools involved in the programme were thoroughly conversant with existing guidelines about child abuse currently in use in their locality. The guidelines recommend ways in which suspected cases of child abuse should be handled, but because the guidelines vary from one area to another it was impractical, in preparation of this manual, to document the extent and precise nature of the variations.

Good communication between all relevant agencies and a clear understanding of the roles and responsibilities of those involved is seen as a vital prerequisite to implementing the *Teenscape* programme. We have therefore included suggestions for setting up an appropriate 'procedure' to deal with information received from young people, suspicion of incidents of sexual abuse and for disclosure from a teenager in case this happens. These suggestions are drawn from experience and should provide a useful and practical basis for establishing or improving a procedure within the school. The suggestions are not given, nor are they intended, to replace or replicate an existing procedure which may be operating within the authority or indeed in the local authority area in which the school exists.

Use

Planning the programme is seen as an essential part of the teaching process. It is important that the whole process, as represented in this manual, is undertaken, so that:

- whoever gives the presentation is confident and familiar with the programme and with the subject of child abuse
- everyone involved with the school understands and supports the initiative
- parents are involved in the teaching of good sense defence to the teenagers so that they can continue the process started by the school.

This unit should be implemented before any attempt to discuss good sense defence with either children or parents is made.

Chapter One – First Steps

This chapter deals with:

- informing the school about the *Teenscape* programme
- identifying the people to be involved in the programme
- organising a meeting of those professionals.

It is divided into two sections:

1. Letting People Know
2. Planning the Meeting

1. Letting People Know

Exactly what steps you need to take will depend on who you are. Although we presume that you are the Headteacher of a school, you may be a teacher or someone not on the staff, such as a school or community liaison officer. You may be a parent and involved with the PTA.

As the Headteacher you may wish to call together some or all of your teachers to discuss the most appropriate way to proceed. This will obviously depend on the size of your school and staff.

The next step is to identify all those people who should be informed of your plans, including the LEA advisors. The programme will not only involve members of the teaching staff. It will involve, and possibly affect, a wide range of people who come into contact with the children at the school. This could include: *Within the school*: secretarial staff, catering staff, maintenance staff, school governors, and parent/teacher associations. (N.B. Informing parents is dealt with in the next unit of this manual.) *Outside the school*: LEA advisors, the police, the social services, the health services, education welfare service, district educational psychologists, the NSPCC (RSPCC/ISPCC), youth workers, play leaders, etc., and local voluntary organisations.

This is not a comprehensive list. There may be other people whom you feel should be informed of the programme.

You may already have contact with representatives of the organisations listed and established ways of working together.

The Need to Know

Forming such a team is an important feature of the *Teenscape* programme. It provides you with a network which you can refer to in the event of a teenager from the school being abused in any way. In this sense, it is a precautionary measure. There are, however, a number of other reasons why these people need to be involved:

- Concern about the problem of child safety has increased rapidly over recent years.
- A range of different agencies is planning to tackle or has tackled the problem iṅ a variety of ways.
- By letting as many relevant agencies as possible know of your plans, you will minimise the risk of unnecessary duplication or confusion.
- Several agencies may be implicated in the procedure you establish in your school for dealing with incidents. They may be agencies that you want to contact or refer young people to.
- There may be agencies who have existing procedures about which you need to be aware.
- A number of people will need to know what the school procedure is, in case a young person or parent reports a case of suspected abuse to them. Teenagers can build up 'special' relationships with any of the adults who work in the school. They might choose to tell the secretary or the dinner lady or the caretaker or the nurse about something that has happened to them.

Some of the people or agencies may be able to help you carry out the programme. This might involve help with reproducing some of the materials, assistance with the running of the parents meetings, the teaching of the lessons, etc.

Invitation List

Having identified all the agencies and groups that you think should be informed of your plans to implement the *Teenscape* programme, draw up a list of individuals from those organisations to be invited to a meeting at the school. This may take some time and effort and you may therefore delegate a small group to do the work, rather than do it all yourself.

Make sure that you get the approriate representative from the larger organisations. It is worth finding out exactly who to send the invitation to, rather than hoping that the letter gets passed on to the right person.

2. Planning the Meeting

Once you have drawn up an invitation list, you can start planning the meeting itself. There are some practical considerations to decide:

- **When** the meeting will take place. What is the most convenient time for the majority of those who will be attending the meeting?
- **Where** the meeting will take place. What is the most suitable room in the school for a meeting of that many people?
- **How long** the meeting should last. How much time is needed to complete all the business? How much time can people give to the meeting?

- **Who** will lead the meeting on the day. Who is the best person to lead the meeting, in terms of commitment, experience and time to prepare? Will minutes be taken, or will you keep some other form of record?

You might not be able to answer all of these questions until you know what the objectives of the meeting are, and what will need to happen to ensure that those objectives are achieved.

Objectives

The objectives for the meeting are as follows:
- To inform people about *Teenscape* and the opportunity it provides to develop a good sense defence programme in the school.
- To learn about any activity by other agencies to tackle the problem of child abuse.
- To plan, in conjunction with other agencies, a programme for teaching good sense defence to students in the school.
- To establish a procedure, if one does not already exist, by which the school can deal with incidents of child abuse.

What Happens in the Meeting

The meeting is divided into four sections:

1. Introduction
2. Information Exchange
3. Teaching Programme
4. School Procedure

These sections are dealt with more fully in the next chapter.
   Teenscape provides a number of resources to help you run the meeting. These are:

- Notes on how to set up a Teaching Programme
- Notes on how to set up a procedure for the school

These are contained in the next chapter.

Preparation

The following suggestions may help:

- study *Teenscape* closely before the meeting and familiarise yourself with:

   — the background information on child abuse
   — what happens in the parents' meeting
   — what happens in the teens' lesson

- plan what you want to say in your introduction. This should include:

   — how long the meeting will last
   — the objectives of the meeting
   — what will happen in the meeting

Further details of what to say in the introductory talk are contained in the next chapter.

- identify any problems that you think may arise when you implement the programme in your school. This might include:
  - difficulties with fitting it into the timetable
  - shortage of staff
  - lack of equipment or resources

You can then ask people at the meeting if they are able to help you overcome these problems.

- establish what guidelines your Education Authority has with specific reference to disclosures of child abuse.

Chapter Two – The Planning Meeting

This chapter deals with:

- running the planning meeting
- planning the teaching programme
- establishing school procedures

It is divided into four sections:

1. Introductory Talk
2. Information Exchange
3. The Teaching Programme
4. School Procedures

1. Introductory Talk

As suggested in the previous chapter, it is a good idea for the person who will be introducing the meeting to prepare what they are going to say beforehand.

The talk should be as short as possible. It should tell people:

- who you are (if necessary)
- what the meeting is for
- what *Teenscape* is
- what will happen in the meeting
- the decisions that must be made by the end of the meeting.

The talk should last no longer than fifteen minutes. The bulk of the information required can be found in different places in this manual.

2. Information Exchange

Ask each of the representatives of outside agencies to:

- state whether they are currently involved in any way with the safety of children
- indicate whether their involvement relates in any way to the issue of child abuse
- explain, if appropriate, the nature of the activity, and how it could relate to the programme.

Any useful information that is obtained from this process should be recorded on a blackboard or flipchart so that it can be referred to throughout the rest of the meeting. It will be especially useful when you come to establish procedures for dealing with incidents or cases of abuse.

To ensure that this part of the meeting does not take up too much time, you may want to:

- brief people before the meeting

- ask them precise questions
- discuss at the start of the meeting how much time you want to spend on this process
- record the key points while they talk

3. The Teaching Programme

There are two basic decisions that need to be made by the meeting before the planning of the teaching programme can progress:

— how best to establish a network which involves all the appropriate agencies/individuals
— how to ensure that the school has a procedure that provides for effective communication between all those involved in the network

Once the procedure has been clarified, the details of the programme can be discussed. These details involve:

A. the timetabling of lessons for students
B. the organisation of meetings for parents
C. the planning of follow-ups to the lessons
D. the teaching of the lesson

A. The Lessons

Details of what is involved in the lessons on good sense defence are contained in the fourth unit of this manual. When the lessons can best be taught will depend on:

— how they can be fitted into the existing school timetable
— how much preparation time is required by the people teaching the lesson

Timetabling

There are two main ways in which the lesson plan can be used. These are not the only ways, but they will give you some idea of how the plan can be adapted:

- The lessons can be used individually or some may be combined. Each section can be dealt with in a separate short period, depending on how much discussion you encourage/allow from the students. The aspect of the lesson are:
  — introduction
  — trusting intuition
  — saying no
  — feeling safe
  — safety when out
  — bullying
  — crime
  — rights and responsibilities
  — relationships

— abuse
— keeping safe from abuse
— getting help/telling someone
— common sense defence
— addiction
— gambling

- The lessons may be taught in weekly blocks or throughout the term or the year, this will depend upon your school timetable

Whichever approach you choose initially, it is recommended that provision be made for some follow-up activities. These will ensure that the lessons are reinforced. This can be done by including secondary activities, which fit in with your ongoing work with a particular class.

Your timetabling of the lessons will depend on what approach you decide to use. It will also depend on the size of group you wish to teach. *Kidscape* recommends that each class be taught on its own, but it is possible, if necessary, to teach the lessons to larger groups.

B. Parents' Meeting

Details of the organisational requirements of the parents' meetings are contained in the third unit of this manual. The decisions that need to be made now are:

- whether to call a parents' meeting
- whether to arrange one meeting for all the parents, or to arrange a series of smaller meetings for different groups of parents (e.g. based on a tutorial group)
- when to arrange the parents' meetings. Each parents' meeting should take place as close to the first *Teenscape* lesson as possible. Ideally, both should take place in the same week, so that the content of the meeting is still fresh in parents' minds when their children come home after the lesson
- who will run the parents' meeting and who will attend. One arrangement which has proved very successful is a combination of the headteacher and those who will be teaching the lesson. The availability of these people will obviously be an important factor in the scheduling of the parents' meetings.

Planning the parents' meetings might cause some slight alterations to your timetabling of the lessons. When you have completed both to the group's satisfaction, write up a rough 'calendar' on the board or flipchart to make sure that people get the correct information, and have a chance to write it down.

C. The 'Teachers'

The lessons do not necessarily have to be taught only by the school's teaching staff. For example, one of the representatives from your network of agencies may want to be actively involved in implementing the programme in your school. This could include: the police; health services; the social services; education welfare service or members of the PTA.

Summary

At this stage in the meeting, you should have decided:

- *Who* will be teaching the lessons
- *When* the lessons will take place
- *Which* lessons you want to use and in what order
- *When* the Parents' Meeting will take place
- *What* kind of follow-up will be provided
- *Who* will be running the Parents' Meeting

4. School Procedures

The school, or the LEA, will already have guidelines laid down for dealing with incidents of child abuse. All those at the meeting need to know about and understand the details of the guidelines.

It may be necessary to clarify the procedure within the school, in the event of either suspicion or disclosure of an incident of abuse.

It is important that everyone is aware of their own role and responsibilities. It is important for everyone to understand how they are involved in the wider 'network' of agencies/individuals invited to the meeting. It will also make them more confident knowing that a procedure exists within the school to support them and any teenager involved in a possible case of abuse.

The procedures need to make clear what to do if any of the adults in the school are made aware that a student is a victim of abuse. This should include:

— who in the school should be given this information and what their responsibilities are
— how it should be recorded
— the contact in the local police force
— the contact in the local social services office
— the contact in the local NSPCC branch
— how to support the victim
— sources of further support and counselling

These are all important elements of the school's procedure which should be known by all those involved with students in the school. You may feel it is advisable to display this information in a prominent position, for example in the staff room.

Appendix 2.1, at the back of this unit, gives examples of procedures which may be of interest. Details dealing with disclosure from both students and adults are given in Units 1, 3 and 4.

It is important to realise that disclosures may also come from colleagues. Over the two-year pilot project, we found that talking about good sense defence, particularly as it related to child abuse, encouraged those involved in running the programme to share their own experiences. Be sensitive to the possibility that people you work with may have suffered abusive experiences when they were children. Discussing the subject now may prompt them to talk about what happened to them. Allow them the same understanding and time that you would to students or parents who might disclose. Should a colleague want to talk, ensure that there is a place for privacy and time to listen. Reading about possible parental disclosure in Unit 3 should be helpful in this situation.

This meeting will have covered some important issues. It will therefore be helpful to those attending the meeting to have a copy of the minutes and the decisions which were taken.

Now turn to Unit 3: The Parents' Meeting. The rest of this manual contains notes for three 'teachers' workshops which may be helpful for those who will be teaching the lesson.

Chapter Three – Teachers' Workshops

This chapter is for use by those who will be teaching teenagers the lessons contained in Unit 4. It deals with:

- the reasons for the workshops
- activities for developing understanding and confidence

It is divided into two sections:

1. Rationale
2. Workshop

Throughout this chapter, the assumption is made that more than one person will be teaching the lessons in your school. If only one person is teaching the lessons, this chapter will still be of use in helping with the preparation.

1. Rationale

There are three main reasons why it is advisable for those people who will be teaching the *Teenscape* lessons to meet together beforehand.

(a)   to increase understanding of and familiarity with the subject of good sense defence
(b)   to increase confidence in tackling the subject of child abuse
(c)   to develop the skills and techniques needed for teaching the lessons

All three of these objectives will be achieved more easily with the support and feedback available from a small group. This can be extended beyond the workshops suggested here. You may find it useful, for example, to meet together after each lesson to compare notes and discuss ways of improving or following up your performance.

(a) Familiarisation

Knowledge of child abuse must also include an understanding of the feelings of the students who have been involved in such incidents.
The exercises in this chapter will help you to:

- familiarise yourself with a young person's perspective on getting help in an adult world
- develop your approach to teenagers who may have experienced some form of abuse

(b) Confidence

You may be feeling anxious about dealing with the subject of good sense defence in the classroom; you may be worried about frightening the students, or about 'taking the lid off a can of worms'! We can assure you, from our own experience, that these fears are groundless. But we are aware that these assurances may not be enough.

By working in a group beforehand, you can:

- share any anxieties that you may be feeling
- talk them through with other people who may be feeling exactly the same
- be reassured by the feedback of colleagues
- prepare strategies for dealing with your anxiety during the lesson

(c) Practise

The plan provided in this manual for the lessons has been developed, refined and proven successful so many times that we know it works.

To ensure that you also get the best results from the programme, you will need to practise teaching the lesson as it is laid out in the lesson plan in Unit 4. For instance:

— there may be parts of the lesson that you want to adapt slightly to suit your teaching style
— there may be techniques, such as roleplay, which you are not familiar with, and will need to develop prior to the lesson
— if you are sharing the lesson with another 'teacher', you will need to co-ordinate each of your contributions. This will require practise to ensure that you don't interrupt each other or have a different understanding of who is doing what.

Resources for a Workshop

The following section of this chapter provides you with resources for a workshop. This focuses on activities which you can use to increase your understanding of the issues and emotions involved.

2. Workshop

This section provides you with a number of activities after some brief notes on preparing for the workshop.

How you organise this workshop will depend on:

- *who* is in the group – for example, you may need to spend some time at the beginning of the workshop getting to know each other better
- *how much* time you have – you may not have time to do all the activities in one workshop
- *how much* space you have – you may only have room to do the activities that don't require any moving around

- *who* is leading the workshop – you may decide to appoint someone to lead the workshop
- *how much* time you may need to spend discussing issues and practicabilities connected with *Teenscape*.

It is best if all the members of the group have an opportunity to read this chapter of the manual prior to the workshop, so that they have an idea of what is likely to happen.

The Activities

Some people may not be used to doing activities like the ones listed overleaf. They may feel uncomfortable, and embarrassed about taking part. The workshop should give people time to settle in and become more relaxed before any of the activities are attempted.

Assure people that they will not be expected to either perform for or repeat personal feelings to the whole group. This will make them more comfortable when they undertake the activities.

One way of starting the workshop is to ask people a general question, for example:

- go round the group asking each person to say briefly how they are feeling about doing the workshop
- go round the group asking each person what they expect to happen in the workshop, what time they have to leave by, etc.

These questions can be useful in clarifying for people what is actually going to happen.

Spend some time discussing each activity after you have done it. The group can then talk over their responses to the activity, and share any memories that it may have evoked.

Activity 1

How can you say that?

This activity give you an understanding of the power that adults have over young people.

- Get into pairs and assume roles as either an adult or a teenager
- The 'teen' tells his/her name to the 'adult'
- The 'adult' denies this statement: 'No it's not; that's not your name; that's not your real name, is it? I know what you're really called; that's just a nickname isn't it? etc.
- The 'teen' tries to convince the 'adult'
- The 'adult' continues to deny that this is true
- After a few minutes swap places and repeat the exercise, so that the 'teen' becomes the 'adult' and vice versa. This time, the 'teen' tells the 'adult' that they are hungry, and the adult denies that this is true

- Discuss the exercise with your partner; describe how it felt and whether it brought back any memories of when you were a child
- In the full group, check whether you ever behave like that to other adults and discuss why you think it is that adults behave to children in this way
- Ask members of the group if anyone can remember a time when they have refused to believe something a child has told them, which later turned out to be true
- Stress that this exercise gives some idea of how difficult it can be for a child to tell someone that an adult has tried to abuse them in any way; and how important it is to teach children to go on telling people until they find someone who will believe them

Activity 2

I've never been so frightened in my life!

This activity explores some of your own childhood memories, and how some memories, though frightening, are remembered almost with affection, whilst others still cannot be laughed off.

Remind the participants that they will not have to share these experiences with the whole group.

- Return to the pairs established for the previous exercise
- Each person is given three minutes to tell of an occasion when they were frightened as a child or a young person. The story should begin with the words: 'I have never been so frightened in my life!' Their partner must not interrupt or say anything until the story has finished.
- When the three minutes are up, the person listening repeats the exercise, telling a true story beginning with the words 'I have never been so frightened in my life!'
- When the second story has finished, the first story-teller should return to their story, and tell their partner whether:
  — the memory still upsets them
  — the incident became a family joke
  — it became the basis of a fear that stayed with them throughout childhood
  — they told anyone about it or kept it a secret

The partner can now ask questions to help the story-teller describe how they feel about the incident now.
- This should then be repeated with the second partner's story.
- Discuss in the full group whether adults take into account the impact that events like these can have on a child's life. Look specifically at how adults react to children who have undergone a frightening experience: do they respect children's feelings; or do they belittle children in the belief that this will help them 'get over it'.

Activity 3

Points of view

This activity is a roleplay of a disclosure situation. It gives you experience of what it is like for a child to tell someone about an incident of sexual abuse; and an opportunity to practice the techniques for dealing with disclosure that are contained at the end of Unit 4.

It is important that each member of the group is thoroughly conversant with the section which deals with disclosure, before this activity is undertaken.

- One person plays the 'child'. Another plays the 'teacher'. A third person watches the interaction and gives feedback to the other two at the end of the roleplay.
- The 'child' has been the victim of an obscene telephone call. S/he has asked to see the 'teacher' after class.
- 'Child' and 'teacher' act out the scene, watched by the observer, who does not interrupt.
- The observer halts the scene when it is not useful to continue it; gives feedback to the 'actors' about what they noticed happening; i.e. by describing what they noticed as closely as possible.
- Repeat this exercise so that all three people have a chance to perform each role at least once.
- In your threesome, discuss the activity in some detail, focusing on:
  — how you felt as the child and teacher
  — what you learnt about the child
  — what you learnt about dealing with disclosure

It is important to allow sufficient time for this discussion in threes.

**Appendix 2.1 –
DES/DHSS
Guidelines**

LAC(88)10
HC(88)38
Welsh Office
Circular/26/88
WHC(88)42

DEPARTMENT OF HEALTH AND SOCIAL SECURITY
AND
WELSH OFFICE

ENGLAND FOR ACTION
To: Chief Executive of
Metropolitan District
Councils
Non-Metropolitan County
Councils
London Borough Councils
Common Council of the City
of London
Council of the Isles of Scilly
Directors of Social Services

Regional Health Authorities
District Health Authorities
Boards of Governors
Community Health Councils
Family Practitioner
Committees (with a copy
for Local Medical
Committees)

WALES FOR ACTION
To: Executive of County Councils
Directors of Social Services:
County Councils

District Health Authorities
Community Health Councils
Family Practitioner
Committees (with a copy
for Local Medical
Committees)

6 July 1988

Working Together for the Protection
of Children From Abuse

SUMMARY

This circular introduces a guide consolidating and updating
existing guidance on inter-agency work in the field of child abuse.
The guide sets this work in the context of the wider statutory
duties of authorities for the health and welfare of children in
their areas and the responsibilities of other bodies concerned. It
outlines the requirements agencies should aim to meet and
recommends administrative, training and other arrangements to
that end. The guide does not offer advice on practice of the
individual professions in their work with children and families.
The circular highlights main points in the guide and some
general points on the prevention of child abuse. The guide has
been prepared following extensive informal consultations by
DHSS and the Welsh Office with staff working at all levels in
services concerned with child protection.

ACTION

Local authorities should:

a.   take the lead in arrangements to redesignate Area Review Committees as Area Child Protection Committees (ACPCs);

b.   ensure local child abuse procedures contain adequate instructions on the taking of place of safety orders.

All authorities and agencies should:

a.   through the ACPCs, review their existing policies and procedures for handling child abuse cases at all levels against the requirements outlined in this circular and the associated guide;

b.   ensure they have in place adequate management information systems;

c.   note the publication of the Report of the Inquiry into Child Abuse in Cleveland 1987 and the Standing Medical Advisory Committee and the Standing Nursing and Midwifery Advisory Committee reports and bring them to the attention of the appropriate staff;

d.   review provision for in-service training and put in hand the establishment of joint training programmes on child abuse issues for professionals in direct contact with children.

Introduction

1.   The protection of children is the proper concern of everyone in a position to help. Primary responsibility for the care and protection of children rests with parents but a range of services are available to help them in this task. Many referrals to agencies are made by parents seeking help for themselves. Relatives, friends and neighbours may also help directly or encourage families to seek help or alert statutory authorities to children about whom they are concerned. All agencies with staff that are in direct contact with children and families must be involved; but those principally concerned are:

Local Social Services Authorities

Health Authorities

Family Practitioner Committees

Local Education Authorities

Police Authorities

Probation Service

NSPCC

Other Voluntary Organisations

2.   Much effort has been made by the statutory authorities and others in recent years to respond to the problem of child abuse and to organise co-operation between services to that end and progress has been achieved. The guide "Working Together - a guide to arrangements for the inter-agency co-operation for the Protection of Children from Abuse" and the other documents referred to later are intended to build on this and secure future improvement. Child abuse work should be given its appropriate priority and sufficient resources made available by the responsible agencies.

Policies and procedures for inter-agency co-operation

3.   Authorities and agencies locally have collaborated extensively in developing policies and procedures for the prevention and management of child abuse. These have included:

a.   establishing Area Review Committees;
b.   setting up of Child Protection Registers, ("At risk registers")
c.   laying down procedures for the handling of cases (particularly regarding inter-disciplinary and inter-agency collaboration); and
d.   introducing arrangements to monitor and review the operation of policies and procedures.

4.   Whilst arrangements have proved their value the guide recommends a range of developments designed to improve their effectiveness; in particular:

a.   Authorities are required to redesignate Area Review Committees as Area Child Protection Committees (ACPCs) and advice is given on the constitution, membership and functions of these committees. Early tasks of the ACPCs should be review existing policies and procedures. ACPCs should make arrangements to receive from constituent agencies the information necessary to enable them to monitor the level and type of activity on child abuse work and to identify trends. The form this should take is a matter for local decision but suggestions are made as to a possible format. It is recommended that an annual report should be prepared by the Committee for the agencies' consideration. That report should be copied to the local Joint Consultative Committees for Health and Social Services for information. The Sercretaries of State also wish to receive copies of such reports for information. A format for reports is suggested.

b.   Investigation into concerns about possible child abuse normally involves co-operation between social services or the NSPCC, the health service and the police. Subsequent assessment and planning will require the nomination by the social services department (or NSPCC) of a key social worker who will carry case responsibility and co-ordinate services being provided to the child and family by all relevant agencies. It is essential that the different agencies are committed by their staff to the plan, and its implications for those agencies understood, if the procedures laid down for the protection and welfare of the child are to be effective in practice. Guidance on the role of the key worker is provided.

c.   All agencies, and particularly social services departments, are asked, where this is not already the case, to assign responsibility to a senior and experienced officer or officers in their organisation to act as a source of expert advice on child abuse work, to promote policy and practice development, and to advise on training needs. Suggestions are made about the functions such staff might discharge.

d.   Authorities should ensure that the status and purpose of meetings and contacts between members of agencies are clear to all concerned. In cases of suspicion or allegation strategy discussions between relevant officers should be held in person or by telephone to decide the strategy for initial investigations in an individual case. A child abuse case conference must be convened to produce and record clear, timely and reasoned recommendations to the agencies providing services. Such case conferences will normally be chaired by a senior officer of the social services department who has experience of child care cases and skills in chairmanship but is not directly involved in supervising the case at fieldwork level. Legal advice should be available whenever required. Guidance is given about the role, organisation and management of case conferences.

e.   Effective child protection depends also on the skills of the professional staff in all relevant disciplines. These are acquired through experience and through basic qualifying training, induction and post qualifying training, in-service or otherwise. Basic qualifying training lies outside the remit of agencies responsible for the management of child abuse and is not addressed in the guide. The guide indicates the need and scope for developing in-service training opportunities, some of which will best be provided or arranged on a joint basis between agencies locally, both in relation to procedural arrangements and professional knowledge and skills. In addition agencies will need to consider their part in providing appropriate practice placements for social work students in child care work and their secondment policies for unqualified staff.

f.   Cases of child sexual abuse should be brought within the system of handling child abuse work generally. The handling of such cases is a comparatively new experience for many staff which requires new knowledge and skills. The guide identifies issues that need to be considered in developing services to meet this challenge.

g.   The existing child abuse registers should continue in being as Child Protection Registers. They should include details of children for whom a plan of action and review is recommended by a case conference. Guidance on the purpose, status and maintenance of the register is provided.

h.   Where cases of abuse occur leading to death or serious injury of a child the ACPC should review the action taken by the agencies and consider whether further inquiry is needed to identify improvements in the local procedure or to restore public confidence.

Involvement of the Public

5.   The public, relatives, friends and neighbours of vulnerable children need to be confident that their concerns, once made know to the local social services departement or the NSPCC, will be acted upon and that the source of the referral will be treated in confidence. The guide recommends that consideration should be given to means of publicising contact points for social services departments, the NSPCC and voluntary groups. The recognition and support by agencies of community help-lines and self-help groups is one way that public awareness and confidence can be enhanced.

Parents

6.   The European Court of Human Rights found the UK Government in breach of Articles 6 and 8 of the European Convention of Human Rights in a recent child care case. Cited as a factor in their considerations was the fact that local authorities had insufficiently involved parents in their decision-making processes. The Report of the Inquiry into Child Abuse in Cleveland 1987 also highlights the need to inform and where appropriate consult parents at each stage of the investigation, to involve them as far as possible in the decision-making process, and to ensure that they are fully informed of the decisions made and their implications and their rights of appeal and complaint. Wherever practical, arrangements for the attendance of parents at case conferences for all or part of the meeting should be made unless in the view of the Chairman their presence would preclude a full and proper consideration of the child's interest. Where allegations or suspicions of abuse prove unfounded this should be made explicitly clear to parents.

7.   Parents should be encouraged to seek help as the prompt and early provision of advice and services can do much to keep families together and to prevent child abuse. When suspicions have been raised it is important to have regard for the anxieties parents may feel.

8.   For so long as it is consistent with the need to protect the child every effort should be made to support and work with the parents and to obtain their co-operation in and support for child protection plans which may be necessary. This always requires that they are kept properly informed of what is intended and why, and their views sought and taken into account.

Children
_____

9.   It is important that throughout investigation and the
subsequent management of cases of child abuse all those working
to protect the child are conscious of how the process may affect
him or her. Points of good practice to remember are set out in the
Report of the Inquiry into Child Abuse in Cleveland 1987 as
follows:-

"a.   Professionals recognise the need for adults to explain to
children what is going on. Children are entitled, to a proper
explanation appropriate to their age, of why they are being
taken away from home and some idea of what is going to
happen to them later.

b.   Professionals should not make promises which cannot be
kept to a child, and in the light of possible court proceedings
should not promise a child that what is said in confidence can
be kept in confidence.

c.   Professionals should always listen carefully to what the
child has to say and take seriously what is said.

d.   Throughout the proceedings the views and the wishes of the
child particularly as to what should happen to him/her should
be taken into consideration by the professionals involved with
their problem.

e.   The views and wishes of the child should be placed before
whichever court deals with the case. We do not however,
suggest that those wishes should predominate.

f.   Children should not be subjected to repeated medical
examinations solely for evidential purposes. Where apropriate
according to age and understanding the consent of the child
should be obtained before any medical examination or
photography.

g.   Children should not be subjected to repeated interviews nor
to the probing and confrontational type of 'disclosure' interview
for the same purpose, for it in itself can be damaging and
harmful to them. The consent of the child should where possible
be obtained before the interviews are recorded on video.

h.   The child should be medically examined and interviewed in
a suitable and sensitive environment, where there are suitably
trained staff available.

i.   When a child is moved from home or between hospital and
foster home it is important that those responsible for the day to
day care of the child not only understand the child's legal status
but also have sufficient information to look after the child
properly.

j. Those involved in investigation of child sexual abuse should make a conscious effort to ensure that they act throughout in the best interests of the child."

Information and Monitoring

10. Arrangements are being made for a new national annual statistical return of numbers on child protection registers. Information from a pilot return as at 31 March 1988 will be published in the autumn (1988).

11. A number of inquiries into child abuse in recent years - of which the Report of the Commission of Inquiry into the circumstances surrounding the death of Kimberley Carlile is the most recent - have identified the need to ensure that agencies maintain adequate records, and that mechanisms exist to facilitate the transfer of information between agencies where appropriate. A further aspect highlighted in the Report of the Inquiry into Child Abuse in Cleveland 1987 is the need to maintain records of activity within agencies on a regular basis, to enable managers to monitor the activities for which they are responsible and to identify potential problems for resolution at an early stage. The guide makes recommendations on the information which should be provided to the ACPC. Agencies are asked to ensure that they have in place management information systems that will enable them to meet these requirements and monitor changes in the level of activity on a regular and frequent basis.

Inquiry into Child Abuse in Cleveland 1987

12. Simultaneously with this circular and accompanying guide the Secretary of State is publishing the Report of the Inquiry into Child Abuse in Cleveland 1987; a summary of the report is issued with this circular. The Report focuses primarily on child sexual abuse, but also is concerned with child abuse generally. Many of its recommendations have been incorporated in the guide "Working Together". Some relate to more detailed issues of professional practice and will be explored further with the relevant professional organisations. In particular the views of the professions will be sought on how the recommendations on Specialist Assessment Teams, referred to in paragraphs 6.11 to 6.13 of Working Together, can best be implemented; and consideration will be given to issuing further guidance if necessary. Other recommendations require legislative changes, and in some cases endorse proposals advanced in the White Paper on the Law on Child Care and Family Services (CM 62) issued in January 1987. That put forward wide-ranging proposals for a major overhaul of child care law, to provide a clearer and fairer framework for the provision of child care services to families and for the protection of children at risk. The effect of the Cleveland Inquiry recommendations are under consideration and the

Government's decisions will be made known in due course. The Government is committed to introduce legislation as soon as the Parliamentary timetable allows.

Place of Safety Orders

13.   The Report of the Inquiry into Child Abuse in Cleveland 1987 recommends that place of safety orders (POSOs) should be sought for the minimum time necessary to ensure protection of the child, that records related to the use of statutory powers on an emergency basis should be kept and monitored regularly by social services departments and that a Code of Practice should be drawn up for the administration of POSOs by social workers, including the provision of information to parents. These recommendations are endorsed by the Secretaries of State. All local child abuse procedures which do not already include this should contain a section setting out in what circumstances POSOs should be sought and how the case should be handled if granted. The Departments will in due course prepare a Code of Practice.

Other relevant guidance

14.   At Ministerial request the Standing Medical Advisory Committee has prepared a report under the aegis of a sub-committee chaired by Professor Eric Stroud on the clinical diagnosis of child sexual abuse. This is being published simultaneously and circulated to all doctors working in the NHS as well as relevant agencies.

15.   At Ministerial request the Standing Nursing and Midwifery Advisory Committee has prepared a report under the aegis of a sub-committee chaired by Miss Suzanne Mowat on advice for nurse managers on child abuse. This is being published simultaneously to relevant agencies.

16.   At the request of Ministers the Social Services Inspectorate of the DHSS have prepared, with the help of a working group chaired by Mr Maurice Phillips, Deputy Chief Inspector, a practice guide for social workers on assessment in child protection cases. This is being piloted in local authorities at present and will be published in October 1988.

17.   The Home Office are publishing simultaneously guidance to the police on the investigation of child sexual abuse - circular HOC52/88. Copies of the guide "Working Together" accompany this.

18.   The Department of Education and Science and the Welsh Office are issuing guidance to education authorities together with the guide "Working Together".

19.   At the request of Ministers the Social Services Inspectorate of the DHSS, in co-operation with the Social Work Service of the

Welsh Office, undertook a national survey in Autumn 1987 of co-operation on child sexual abuse matters between the local authorities, police, health services and the NSPCC, as seen from the perspective of social services departments. This is being published simultaneously and circulated to relevant agencies.

Training

20.   The Secretaries of State have recognised the importance of training of managers and practitioners in child abuse working and a central initiative was launched in October 1986. The initiative consists of seven projects at present. Details are given in Annex A. Information about each project as it comes to fruition will be made available separately. The Inquiry into Child Abuse in Cleveland 1987 reported that training was one of the major needs identified and indicated that it is urgent to give in-service training to professionals to bring them up to date on child sexual abuse matters. More specialised training and inter-agency training are recommended. Agencies are asked to review their provision for single discipline and multi-disciplinary in-service training and to put in hand the establishment of joint training programmes.

21.   The Government accepts that urgent action can and should be taken to improve and extend training. Accordingly it has decided to extend the Training Support Programme for Social Services Departments to the child care field. A grant of 70% in support of expenditure of £10m will be made available in England for the purpose in 1989/90. Discussions will be started immediately with the local authority associations and other interested bodies to ensure that an effective programme can be put in place by then. Appropriate complementary arrangements are in hand in Wales.

Resources

22.   The rate support grant settlement for 1987/88 and 1988/89 took into account estimates of the additional resources needed to enable local authorities to cope with increased work on child abuse, including extra expenditure on training of social services staff. The settlement for 1989/90 has yet to be determined. Individual local authorities will need to consider the resources required to implement the guidance in this circular in the light of local circumstances and priorities.

Circulars Withdrawn

23.   In England: LASSL (74)13, CMO (74)8; LASSL (74)5 -; LASSL (76)2, CMO (76)2, CNO (76)3; LASSL (80)4, HN (80)20. In Wales: Instructions will be issued in due course.

24.   Any enquiries about this circular should be addressed to Community Services Division (CS3A) DHSS or HSSPI Division Welsh Office.

R P S Hughes
Department of Health and
  Social Security

Community Services (CS3A)
Department of Health and
  Social Security
Alexander Fleming House
Elephant and Castle
London SE1 6BY
01-407-5522 Ext 6284

R J Davies
Welsh Office

HSSPI Division
Welsh Office
Cathays Park
Cardiff
CF1 3NQ
0222 823145

Further copies of this circular and the guidance "Working Together" may be obtained (by written request) from DHSS Store, Health Publications Unit, No 2 Site, Manchester Road, Heywood, Lancs., OL10 2PZ quoting code and serial number appearing at top right-hand corner.

Circular No 4/88
6 July 1988

DEPARTMENT OF EDUCATION AND SCIENCE
ELIZABETH HOUSE
YORK ROAD
LONDON SE1 7PH

To: Local Education Authorities
    All maintained schools
    Other bodies

WORKING TOGETHER FOR THE PROTECTION OF CHILDREN FROM
ABUSE: PROCEDURES WITHIN THE EDUCATION SERVICE

INTRODUCTION

1. There is increasing concern about child abuse generally, and
specifically in relation to the report of the Inquiry into Child Abuse in
Cleveland. The Secretary of State wishes to secure effective
arrangements so that everyone who is in a position to help to protect
abused children, or children at risk of abuse, is enabled to do so
effectively, whatever his or her relationship to the children concerned.
The DHSS Circular LAC(88)10 and Guide entitled "Working Together",
copies of which are enclosed with this Circular, emphasise the
importance of, and provide guidance on, cooperation between the
agencies concerned with the protection of children. This Circular
accordingly provides advice on action which should be taken within the
education service to enable cases of suspected or identified abuse to
be properly considered and pursued.

2. Primary responsibility for the protection of children from abuse rests
with the local authorities' Social Services Departments (SSDs). The
NSPCC and the police also have statutory responsibilities, and they with
SSDs and health authorities are the principal agencies involved in
investigating and dealing with individual cases. In addition to the
education service, others whose contacts with young people put them in
a position to help include family practitioner services, probation services,
local authority housing departments, local social security offices, the
Armed Forces where the families of Service personnel are concerned,
and voluntary and church organisations.

3. In brief, the principal recommendations of this Circular are for:

    — each LEA to designate a senior official as having LEA-wide
      responsibility for coordinating policy and action; to review its
      procedures; to ensure that its procedures are set out in a widely-
      available document; and to develop appropriate arrangements for
      in-service training;

    — each school to designate a senior member of staff as having
      responsibility, under the procedures established by the LEA, for
      coordinating action within the school and for liaison with other
      agencies.

4.   The term "child abuse" is defined in "Working Together". It includes physical injury, neglect including emotional neglect, continued ill-treatment and sexual abuse.

INDICATIONS OF ABUSE

5.   Because they are in regular and frequent contact with children, school staff are particularly well placed to observe outward signs of abuse, or unexplained changes in behaviour or performance which may indicate abuse. Bruises, lacerations and burns may be apparent, particularly when children change their clothes for physical education and sports activities. Possible indicators of physical neglect, such as inadequate clothing, poor growth, hunger or apparently deficient nutrition, and of emotional neglect, such as excessive dependence or attention-seeking, may be noticeable. Sexual abuse may exhibit physical signs, or lead to a substantial behavioural change including precocity or withdrawal. These signs and others can do no more than give rise to suspicion – they are not in themeselve proof that abuse has occurred. But as part of their pastoral responsibilities teachers should be alert to all such signs. The designation of a coordinating teacher should not be seen as diminishing the role of all teachers in being alert to signs of abuse.

6.   Where teachers see signs which cause them concern they may have the opportunity to seek information from the child, with tact and sympathy. If not, or if the child's responses do not dispel suspicion, teachers should immediately make their concern known to the senior member of staff with specific designated responsibility.

7.   Other school staff should similarly report any suspicions they may have.

8.   Care must be taken in interpreting children's responses to questions about indications of abuse. Abused children may have been told by the abuser what to say in response to questions, and may have been threatened. The abuser may be a close relative. It is not the responsibility of school staff to make enquiries of parents or guardians, and in some cases it could be counter-productive for them to do so. It is for the statutory agencies — SSDs, the NSPCC and the police — to investigate suspected abuse. School staff should not take action beyond that set out in the LEAs procedures. But information may sometimes be volunteered to staff in the course of conversation, especially in a school which has positive and regular contact with parents. If a parent or guardian volunteers information it should be recorded.

9.   It should be noted that it is rare for children, and in particular young children, to make false accusations of sexual abuse. Where a child alleges that he or she is being sexually abused this should be taken seriously and deemed to merit investigation. If the allegation is subsequently found to be false it may nevertheless be an indication of a child's need for help in other ways.

REPORTING OF SUSPECTED ABUSE

10.   In all cases where teachers, or other members of staff, consider that they have good cause to suspect abuse — including neglect, and emotional ill-treatment — they should report their suspicions to a senior member of staff to whom has been given responsibility for coordinating the school's response to child abuse. This may be the headteacher or another senior teacher. He or she should then follow the procedures laid down by the local education authority for reporting such cases. These procedures should entail contacting a named member of the local Social Services Department and informing a named officer of the Education Department. They may also entail informing the Chairman of the school's Governing Body. The procedures should include provision for emergency action, including action to give immediate protection to the child where necessary and instructions for dealing with cases when the staff normally responsible are unavailable.

11.   The same procedures should be followed when information about abuse is volunteered to a member of staff by the child concerned. This may sometimes be done obliquely rather then directly. An abused child is likely to be under severe emotional stress, and the staff member may be the only adult whom the child is prepared to trust. When information is offered in confidence, the member of staff will need tact and sensitivity in responding to the disclosure. The member of staff will need to reassure the child, and retain his or her trust, while explaining the need for action, which will necessarily involve other adults being informed. It will call for an understanding not only of the child's own ambivalent feelings but also of the staff member's own feelings about child abuse.

12.   In some cases Education Welfare Officers will be the first to identify possible abuse. They should inform the designated senior member of staff of the school concerned as well as their own senior management, and the case should then be dealt with in accordance with the local education authority's procedures. Where the school itself identifies a possible case of abuse the Education Welfare Office may be able to advise on a child's home circumstances.

13.   Information indicating that a child is at risk of abuse should also be reported through the authority's procedures, even when there is no indication that the child in question has yet suffered.

14.   If child abuse is suspected, it will be essential to have a record of all the information available. Staff should note carefully what they have observed and when they observed it. Signs of physical injury should be described in detail, or sketched. Any comment by the child concerned, or by an adult who might be the abuser, about how an injury occurred should be recorded, preferably quoting words actually used, as soon as possible after the comment has been made.

CHILD ABUSE WITHIN THE SCHOOL

15.   It is regrettably the case that some teachers and other members of school staff have in the past been found to have committed child abuse.

Such incidents are rare; but, not least because they represent a breach of trust, it is vital that a suspicion that a staff member has been involved in the abuse of a child should be reported to the headteacher. The local education authority should be consulted and its documented procedures followed. In the exceptional case where the headteacher is suspected, the staff member who is made aware of the possible offence should report it to the deputy headteacher who in turn should report to the LEA, whose procedures again should be followed.

CHILDREN WITH SPECIAL EDUCATIONAL NEEDS

16.   Indications of child abuse concerning children with special educational needs should be reported exactly as they would for other children. But since a school's relationship with the family are especially important where a child has special needs, subsequent dealings with and expectations of parents should be handled with particular care.

LIAISON BETWEEN SCHOOLS AND SOCIAL SERVICES DEPARTMENTS

17.   Social Services Departments have been asked by DHSS to pass on promptly to schools details of children known to be on the Child Protection Register. These details should include the care status of the child and where possible such information as has been made known to the parents about any allegations or suspicions of abuse. Schools are asked to pay particular attention to the attendance and development of all such children and to report any cause for further concern. It is important also that where a child moves school the information is passed on to the new school. SSDs are asked, in turn, to inform schools of any decision to remove a child from the Child Protection Register and of any termination of a care order, as well as any change in the status or the placement of the child.

18.   SSDs are being asked to redesignate Area Review Committees as Area Child Protection Committees and to ensure that such Committees include representatives of the LEA and of the teaching profession.

19.   This Circular asks each LEA to designate a senior official as having LEA-wide responsibility for coordinating policy and action, including liaison at LEA level with the SSD and other agencies. To ensure proper liaison at the level of the school, on individual cases, it is important that schools enable the appropriate teacher to participate fully in case conferences. This may be the headteacher or the senior teacher with designated responsibility, or another member of staff, depending on the school's assessment of which member of staff is best placed to contribute effectively to discussion of the child's welfare. The LEA's documented procedures should give guidance to schools.

THE CONTRIBUTION OF THE CURRICULUM

20.   In the longer term schools may be able to play a part in the prevention of child abuse through the teaching they offer. Courses in personal and social education can help young people to develop more realistic attitudes towards the responsibilities of adult life, including

parenthood. Some schools provide courses in practical child care skills, which may contribute towards better parenting. But LEAs, school governors and schools themselves will wish to consider carefully the extent to which teaching should be more directly concerned with warning children of the risks of child abuse, including sexual abuse, and with helping them to protect themselves. In the light of the Education (No 2) Act 1986 school governors will need to consider whether and if so how they wish the curriculum to include education about sexual abuse. Any subsequent decisions on materials and the development of programmes appropriate to the level of maturity of the children concerned will be a matter of sensitive professional judgement. Though gains can be made in preventing abuse, these must be balanced against the risks of causing anxiety and of undermining stable family relationships. Guidance on the implications of Sections 18 and 46 of the Education (No 2) Act 1986 for sex education at school is given in DES Circular 11/87.

THE YOUTH SERVICE

21. Youth and Community Workers (YCWs) also have close contacts with children and young people, and they too should be alert for signs of abuse. Much youth work depends for its effectiveness on the quality of individual relationships based on confidentiality, but ultimately the appropriate agencies must be informed of suspected or identified abuse. Like school staff, YCWs will need tact and sensitivity to maintain a young person's trust whilst providing for his or her safety. LEAs should define in documented procedures the circumstances in which YVWs should consult colleagues, line managers, and other statutory authorities, recognising the importance of maintaining confidentiality between the young person and the YCW so far as is consistent with safety.

EDUCATION OF ADULTS

22. LEAs should consider the extent to which, within their responsibilities for adult, further and higher education, there is scope for personal and social education about the prevention of child abuse. In addition, adult students may disclose to their teachers that they had suffered abuse as children, and LEAs should consider whether their documented procedures should include guidance on local sources of help and counselling for such students.

TRAINING

23. The criteria governing all courses of initial teacher training include the requirement that students should be prepared for their pastoral responsibilities as teachers. Acknowledging the many pressures on curriculum time in initial training, the Secretary of State nevertheless expects that this preparation will include awareness and recognition of child abuse, and the appropriate procedures as outlined in this Circular.

24. In-service training will be needed for those senior teachers designated as having special responsibility for liaison and for coordination of action within the school. Such training should provide for

awareness and recognition of child abuse, detailed knowledge of the LEA's procedures for dealing with individual cases, and the indentification of those officers withing the statutory agencies with whom the teacher may need to liaise. In devising training programmes LEAs should consult the local SSD; some training may be best be provided on an inter-agency basis.

25.   Where LEAs, governors and schools wish to include a curricular element — as discussed in paragraph 20 above — this will have in-service training implications for those teachers charged with its delivery. Unless such teachers have already had the necessary training LEAs will need to adjust their in-service training programmes to enable them to become aware of pupils' needs in this field, both curricular and pastoral, as well as to familiarise them with the materials to be used.

26.   In addition, LEAs may wish to enable training to be provided to all school staff on awareness and recognition of child abuse. They will wish staff to know of the designation of a senior teacher within each school as coordinator and liaison point, and to have brought to their attention the LEA's documented procedures. Such information could be provided at school, by the designated teacher following his or her in-service training and in consultation with the LEA's designated coordinating officer, or by one of the other major agencies involved. Similar considerations apply to the Youth Service.

27.   Where an addition is involved to LEAs' present arrangements for in-service training on the protection of children from abuse, they will need to consider this against other local priorities within their allocations under the LEA Training Grants Scheme. It is not intended that significant net additional costs should be incurred.

ACTION BY LOCAL EDUCATION AUTHORITIES

28.   The Secretary of State is aware that some local education authorities have already acted to help to protect children through providing guidance and training for their staff. He asks that all LEAs should:

  a. immediately review the effectiveness of their existing arrangements for dealing with child abuse in the light of this Circular and the DHSS Circular and Guide, "Working Together", enclosed;

  b. draw up in consultation with the local Social Services Department a document setting out specific procedures for dealing with individual cases. This document should be brought to the attention of all staff in schools and other relevant personnel, and new staff should be made aware of it on appointment. Where such a document already exists, it should be reviewed. The procedures should be reviewed from time to time;

  c. identify a senior office of the authority as having responsibility for coordinating policy and action on child abuse in schools and the Youth Service throughout the LEA, and as the point of contact with the local Social Services Department and other agencies;

d. give to the headteacher or another senior member of staff in every school, responsibility for liaising with the authority and with the local Social Services Department and other agencies on individual cases of suspected or identified child abuse, acting as the contact point within the school. The designated member of staff should be responsible for coordinating action within the school on child abuse, including liaising with other staff who have designated responsibilities for pastoral care; and, where appropriate, for overseeing the planning of any curricular provision. For the Youth Service, the Principal Youth Officer or another senior officer should be given a similar responsibility;

e. draw up and distribute separate guidance for Youth and Community Workers;

f. consider the suggestions for the education of adults in paragraph 22 above;

g. develop arrangements for the appropriate in-service training of teachers and other staff as outlined in paragraphs 24–27 above, in liaison with the local Social Services Department and on an inter-agency basis where practicable.

29.   The Secretary of State intends, in a year's time, to review the arrangements made by LEAs for giving effect to the recommendations in this Circular.

RESOURCES

30.   The recommendations made in this Circular are designed to help LEAs and schools to increase the effectiveness of their efforts to prevent and deal with child abuse. The recommendations should not have significant additional financial or manpower consequences.

D J S HANCOCK

**Appendix 2.2 –
Incident Log**

Date ....

Date of incident...

Time of indident ....

Person reporting..

Address ....

....

Telephone ....

Relationship to school ....

Details of incident (location etc.)...

....

....

....

....

....

....

....

Referred to (person/agency concerned)..   Date......................

Action taken ....

....

....

....

....

....

....

....

....
Name of person completing report   Signature

Unit 3 | The Parents' Meeting

Planning and running parents' meetings to explain the teaching programme.

Introduction

This unit explains how to organise and run a meeting for parents. The purpose of the parents' meeting is:

- to explain the *Teenscape* 'Good Sense Defence' programme
- to explain why you plan to teach good sense defence to their children
- to explain what will be involved in that process

It has been shown that the most effective way of teaching prevention techniques is by enlisting the support and active involvement of parents.

Throughout the unit, reference is made to 'parents'. 'Parents' here means any adult or adults with whom the child is living, and who are responsible for the child's welfare.

Use

The parents' meeting is seen as an essential part of the process of teaching good sense defence.

This unit should be put into operation at the point indicated in Unit 1; after the Planning Meeting and before the Lessons for teenagers.

Contents

This unit is divided into three chapters:

Chapter One – Preparing the Meeting
The steps that need to be taken to set up the parents' meeting

Chapter Two – Running the Meeting
Step-by-step plan of what to do in the meeting itself – includes the basis for a talk to be given to parents

Chapter Three – After the Meeting
Possible issues that may arise from the meeting – needs for
reassurance, or advice, that might be voiced by parents

Appendix 3.1 – Common Adult Concerns
Questions which might be asked at the end of the meeting, with
some suggested answers

Appendix 3.2 – Letter to Parents

Appendix 3.3 – Leaflet
'Good Sense Defence' A Programme for Your Child's Protection

Appendix 3.4 – Leaflet
'Child Sexual Abuse'

Chapter One – Preparing the Meeting

This chapter deals with:

- the method for contacting parents to inform them of the meeting
- the tasks involved in organising the meeting
- the preparation required for the introductory talk

It is divided into three sections:

1. Making Contact
2. Time and Place
3. The Introductory Talk

1. Making Contact
Who and When

At the Planning Meeting (see Unit 2), you will have decided:

- how many students are going to be involved in each lesson
- when each group is to be taught
- who is going to do the teaching

These decisions will affect how you set about contacting the parents. For example, you may decide to have:

- one meeting for the parents of all the children in the school
- separate meetings for the parents of all the children in one year
- separate meetings for the parents of the children from one particular class or tutorial group

Bear in mind that however many parents are coming to the meeting, it is preferable that more than one person is there to help run it.

Process

In Appendix 3.2 we have provided you with a sample of a suggested letter layout to send to parents which notifies them of the meeting. This sample can be reproduced on to the school's headed notepaper if you wish. Alternatively, you may wish to design your own letter. Whichever method you choose, the letter should contain the following:

— an explanation of the purpose of the parents' meeting
— a return slip for parents to fill in to let you know whether they are coming to the meeting

We have provided samples (Appendices 3.3 and 3.4) of two leaflets for parents which could accompany the letter or be handed out at the parents' meeting. The leaflet entitled 'A Programme for Your Child's Protection' explains the concept of 'Good Sense Defence' and tells parents about the content of the

lessons in which children will be involved. The leaflet entitled
'Child Sexual Abuse' gives facts, danger signs and what to do if a
child tells about abuse. These leaflets can be photocopied.

Once the letters have been reproduced, they should ideally be
posted to the parents. They could be given to the students to
take home, but this creates the risk of them not being delivered.

Hopefully, all the parents will return the slip indicating that
they intend to come to the meeting. It is possible, however, that
some parents will not respond to the letter at all. This could be
for a number of reasons: it might not mean that the parents are
not interested.

You will have to decide if you have the time and resources to:

- contact any parents who have not sent back the return slip
- send home another copy of the letter with a hand-written note
  explaining that you would appreciate their response.

If parents either don't respond, or can't come to the meeting that
you have arranged, you may want to:

- invite them to meetings you are organising for other groups of
  parents
- organise another meeting for those parents if the numbers
  warrant this and if you have time
- go ahead with the programme with the approval of the school
  governors.

2. Time and Place

When and where the meeting happens are important factors,
they determine how many parents come to the meeting and how
comfortable they feel when they get there.

When

The parents' meeting should ideally be organised in the week
before you plan to begin teaching *Teenscape*. If this cannot be
arranged, try to ensure that the parents' meeting happens as
close to the first lesson as possible, so that the information is
still fresh in the parents' minds. This makes it easier for parents
to reinforce the messages at home.

Where

Where you hold the meeting will depend on how many parents
are coming. You will know best what rooms you have available to
hold different size groups. Because of the sensitivity of the
subject, however, we would like to make the following
recommendations:

— the smaller the room the better, as long as there is room for
  everybody. Smaller rooms make for a more relaxed
  atmosphere
— make the room as comfortable as possible: for example, soft
  chairs rather than hard ones, if there are enough to go
  round

— if possible, have hot drinks available for people as they come in. This will help them relax and give them something to focus on while they wait for the meeting to start

— it can also be useful to provide hot drinks at the end of the meeting as it encourages an informal atmosphere at a time when parents may wish to talk to you.

3. Introductory Talk

The plan of the meeting in the next chapter includes a framework for a talk to be given at the beginning of the parents' meeting. This framework is based on the model used by KIDSCAPE in the many presentations given to groups of parents. The talk should last no longer than 15 minutes.

The framework provides all the necessary information to be included in the talk. Whoever gives the talk will need to spend some time preparing it prior to the meeting, in the ways suggested below:

• Read through the framework, the Introductory Talk.
• Decide how best to use the framework. These are examples of ways it could be used:
    — as notes for you to refer to during the meeting
    — as the basis for a speech that you write out before the meeting
    — as the basis for a talk that you improvise during the meeting.
• Practise giving your talk before the meeting, so that you can sort out any problems that you may not have anticipated.
• Try your talk out on friends or colleagues prior to the meeting. They will be able to give you feedback on whether the presentation is clear and intelligible. Their reaction may also give you some idea of how parents are likely to react and the possible questions they may ask at the end of the meeting.

Describing the
Lessons

Later on in the parents' meeting you will need to describe what happens in the lessons.

A summary of the main messages that are taught in the lessons is included in one of the leaflets and in Section 5 of the next chapter (pages 74–75).

When you have looked at the parents' letter and the leaflets, return to this manual and read the following chapter: Running the Parents' Meeting.

Chapter Two – Running the Parents' Meeting

This chapter is a step-by-step guide to running the meeting itself.

The chapter is divided into seven sections:

1. What happens at the Meeting
2. Starting the Meeting
3. Talk for Parents
4. Summary of the Lessons
5. Questions and Answers
6. Parental Feedback
7. Ending the Meeting

If you have not read the first chapter of this manual, which deals with the preparation for the meeting, you should do so now.

1. What Happens at the Meeting

The meeting consists of three main parts:

— an introductory talk
— summary of the lessons
— a question and answer session

What Needs to be Done?

There are a number of tasks involved in running the meeting. We suggest that if possible these tasks are shared amongst a number of people who will run the meeting. They will need to:

• give the introductory talk
• summarise the lessons
• invite and try to answer the parents' questions

What do we Provide?

The talk, the summary, the parents' letter, the two leaflets and the list of questions are provided in this manual.

After the Meeting

Some parents might want to speak to you after the meeting, or arrange to come to see you at a future date. The third chapter of this manual gives guidelines for dealing with such eventualities.

2. Starting the Meeting

Most, if not all, of the parents attending the meeting will be pleased that the school has taken the initiative of setting up the good sense defence programme. However, the whole subject of children's safety can engender strong feelings, particularly the issue of child abuse.

Parents attending the meeting will probably be feeling curious, defensive or apprehensive, about the meeting ahead. Try and put yourself in their shoes for a minute; what would you be feeling?

It is also a possibility that some of the parents might themselves have had abusive experiences.

It is important, therefore, that the meeting starts off on the right foot. Parents will need to be encouraged to feel comfortable and relaxed as soon as possible. They will need to be reassured that the meeting isn't going to be 'difficult' or embarrassing.

As People Come in

How you greet the parents as they come in will contribute to how they feel about the meeting:

- **try to make contact with each person as they come through the door**
  With two (or more) people running the meeting, one of you can position yourself by the door, whilst the other can stay in the middle of the room to make sure that everybody has been personally greeted.

- **have available extra copies of the leaflets**
  Since not everybody will arrive at the meeting at the same time, these leaflets will give people something to focus on if they don't want to make contact with other people.

Making a Start

When you are ready to start the meeting, make sure someone stays by the door to welcome any latecomers and to show them to a seat.

In starting the meeting you should:

- thank everybody for coming
- introduce yourself
- introduce any members of staff present
- introduce anyone attending the meeting representing an agency or organisation involved in the programme
- make sure everybody has got the leaflets and has had time to look through them.

When everybody is ready, explain what is going to happen during the meeting:

- that you are going to talk to them for about 15 minutes
- that you will summarise the lessons
- that you will then try to answer any questions that they might wish to ask – stress that you would like people to save their questions until the end
- that, at the end of the meeting, you will ask the parents for their opinions about teaching *Teenscape*
- that you will stay behind for a specified amount of time after the meeting to see any parents who might want to talk with you

Before you start the introductory talk, make sure that everybody can see and hear you clearly.

3. Talk for Parents
Using the Text

The text of the talk for parents has been broken down into note form, which has worked well for most schools. You can read it as it is or use it as a framework from which to devise your own presentation.

At the beginning of each part of the presentation we have included quotes to give you a sense of how the information can be communicated.

In the right-hand margin, we have included notes and statistics which you may wish to use in your presentation. Some of these are drawn from other parts of the manual. Others are anecdotes gained from experience of using the programme. They have been placed where we think they could be introduced if you use them. The place is indicated by an ⟶ sign in the notes. The numbers refer to References in Unit 1.

Text

'We are here to talk about how to help young people understand and develop strategies about avoiding dangers such as muggings, bullying, abuse, gambling and other addictive behaviours, as well as learning about crime, their rights and responsibilities, and trusting their own intuition to get away and get help.'

- As children grow up they have to learn to deal with many different problems. ⟶

  Kidscape teaches teens 'Good Sense Defence'.

- Most young people at some time, will find themselves in a frightening situation.
- *Kidscape* helps young people deal with these problems by giving them strategies.
- Telling and getting help are key elements. Teaching teens to make a fuss and get away are important, but teaching *Kidscape* strategies does not absolve adults of the responsibility for children's safety ⟶

  'Good Sense Defence' is child-centred, but its success depends upon everyone in the community being involved.

- Teenagers will also discuss
  their right to be safe and
  their responsibilities to
  themselves and others. This
  is an important way for them
  to understand what
  citizenship is about.
- So the *Kidscape* programme
  is about safety,
  responsibilities and co-
  operation.
- You are all probably familiar
  with the problem of bullying
  or keeping safe while
  travelling in public places.
  But the problem of abuse
  can be more difficult to
  understand.

'Many of us are likely to be unclear about what is meant by child
abuse. There are different forms of child abuse: physical,
emotional, sexual and neglect. Because so many people are
concerned about the problem of child sexual abuse, let's begin
by considering what it is.'

- There are several definitions
  of child sexual abuse.
- Generally it is the
  exploitation of a child under
  the age of 16 for the sexual
  gratification of an older
  person.
- It covers a wide range of
  offences $\longrightarrow$

  'flashing'
  obscene phone calls
  pornographic photographs
  fondling
  rape
  indecent assault
  incest.

- It can be one incident or a
  series of events which occurs
  over a number of years.
- Child sexual abuse occurs
  when a child is unable to
  give informed consent.

'It is quite possible that there are people here who were abused
as children. There may also be parents here whose children may
have had abusive experiences. Let us all be sensitive to that
possibility.'

- Sexual abuse is not a new problem.
- However, public awareness of the problem is new.
- This is reflected in the amount of recent media coverage.
- This growing awareness and concern has encouraged people to tell about what happened when they were children.
- More and more people are talking about their experiences, so it seems like the problem is growing. We do not know if it is or if the reported cases are increasing.

'Because the effects of child sexual abuse are often not immediately visible, many adults think that 'no real harm' has been done.'

- Sexually abusive experiences can result in real harm.
- Sexual abuse can seriously affect how people develop.
- Child sexual abuse can lead to and be a cause of addictive behaviour —→

There is evidence that being abused as a child can lead to addiction to drugs, solvents or alcohol. (11)

- It can lead to emotional and psychological disorders.
- Child sexual abuse can lead to disturbed sexual behaviour in adult life.
- It can result in the victim growing up to become an offender —→

In one study of offenders in a prison in the US, 80% had been abused themselves as children. (14)

- The effects of child sexual abuse can be further compounded if the child found any part of the experience pleasurable —→

If a child responds physically to sexual abuse, it is not the fault of the child. This reaction makes it even more difficult to cope with the abuse as the child can feel betrayed by his or her own body. (1)

- It is important to stress that many survivors of child sexual abuse grow up to be loving and caring individuals.

'In 75% of the reported cases of child sexual abuse in Britain, the offender was known to the child'

- Although teens are often over-confident, we must continue to warn them about the dangers of strangers.
- But this is not enough ⟶

Just teaching children to beware of strangers is like teaching them to only watch for red cars when they cross the road. (1)

- Only a minority of offenders are 'strangers'.
- Most offenders are known to the children they abuse ⟶

A report published in 1982 claims that 75% of offenders were known to the victim. (15) Another, the same year, claimed 90%. (4)

- Many children don't know what a stranger is ⟶

Sometimes teenagers can be confused. One reported that strangers were 'brown mac jobs'!

The *Kidscape* pilot project had thousands of answers from children on the subject of 'What is a stranger?'. Many children replied that strangers:

— are ugly
— wear masks
— smell
— have beards
— wear dark glasses
— are always men

One child from a small village said 'I suppose there must be a stranger somewhere on this earth.' We have been warning children for years about strangers, but many are still looking for the 'weird man in the dirty raincoat'.

'Even if the statistics are not exact, we are still faced with the fact that children are being sexual abused. One child is one too many'.

- It is estimated that 1 in 10 British adults have had a sexually abusive experience as a child.
- This includes boys, as well as girls ⟶

These statistics come from the MORI poll in 1984 – 12% of women asked and 8% of men had had a sexually abusive experience before the age of 16. The reported experiences ranged from obscene comments to flashing to rape.

- Sexual abuse does not mean only intercourse. Statistics do indicate that 1 in 10 children may come into contact with someone who will behave in a sexually inappropriate way towards them.
- We should also remember that it can be very frightening for a child to receive an obscene telephone call or to be flashed at by a stranger, but to be sexually abused by someone they know like a neighbour, friend or relative can be completely devastating.

'The vast majority of *reported* offenders are men, many are married with children of their own, some will have been abused themselves as children. We know less about women abusers. There are reported cases but far fewer than reported cases of men abusers'.

- Offenders come from all walks of life and all trades and all professions.
- One feature that offenders share is that they are good at

making sure that children
don't tell on them.
- They use threats, bribes, and
  the authority of being an
  adult to force children to
  keep quiet.
- It is estimated that on
  average an offender will have
  abused 75 children before he
  is caught →

This figure comes from a study
carried out by Columbia
University. (16)

'One of the most important messages that we can teach young
people is to tell and keep telling until someone believes and
helps them'.

- We must encourage them to
  tell us when they feel
  frightened or uncomfortable.
- Teenagers won't always be
  able to be direct; they may
  feel uncomfortable or
  ashamed, or be unable to
  explain what has happened.
- We must learn to listen to
  what they are saying to us,
  and be sensitive to the signs
  that they give.
- Children and young people
  rarely lie about sexual abuse
  →

Very few young people actually
make up these incidents. If
they do, they have a problem
which must be addressed.

- We must start from a
  position of believing the
  child. Better to trust them
  than to dismiss their story
  and be proved wrong.

We also realise that it is important not to over-react and find
abuse everywhere. Most children are not abused and *Teenscape*
is not only about prevention of abuse.

Teenscape gives young people strategies without frightening
them. The approach is low-key, matter-of-fact and non-
sensational, whether dealing with issues of abuse or bullying or
saying no.

- Students are taught to trust
  their own instincts when
  anyone touches them in a

way which makes them feel uncomfortable or which is secretive.

- *Teenscape* teaches them that it is OK to say 'No' to anyone who asks them to do anything that does not feel right.
- *Teenscape* encourages young people to tell if they have any kind of problem →

Teens often tell a friend or Gran or other relative. It might be a good idea to tell Grans about *Teenscape.*

- No-one can keep children safe all the time. Sometimes it is not possible to say no or tell. But our children deserve the right to strategies which will enable them to use their judgement to help protect themselves, if at all possible.

4. Summary of Lessons

You may now wish to summarise the lessons and describe in more detail the way in which your school intends to run and present the lessons. (Remember that Leaflet 1 also contains a summary of the *Kidscape* 'Good Sense Defence' Programme.)

Introduction
Trusting Intuition
Saying No
Feeling Safe
Safety When Out
Bullying
Crime
Rights and Responsibilities
Relationships
Abuse
Keeping Safe From Abuse
Getting Help/Telling Someone
Common Sense Defence
Addiction
Gambling

The introduction to the students begins by explaining that they will be exploring issues around personal safety and how to say no and get help in a variety of potentially difficult situations. The students will be asked about their concerns and there will be groundrules agreed for the discussions.

The subsequent lessons will involve the students in activities. For example, during many of the lessons the students will be making up roleplays or designing questionnaires to talk about attitudes to such things as bullying. They will practise some skills such as getting out of a hold or shouting 'No' to get help. They may do projects to find out what kind of help is available locally. 'What If' questions will be discussed to help them think about what they would do if confronted by a situation such as missing the last bus home or being approached by someone demanding money.

At all times, getting away and getting help are stressed as the best options, if possible. We believe that personal safety is more important than being macho or fighting to keep possessions. The only time to fight back is if there is absolutely no other choice.

Teenscape is not trying to turn teenagers into self-defence experts, but is trying to get them to use common sense.

If any parent would like to see a copy of the lessons themselves, please let me know and I will be pleased to arrange it.

5. Questions and Answers

Tell parents that you will now try to answer any questions that they want to ask. Remind them that you are staying behind after the meeting, and will be happy to see anybody who wants to talk with you then.

Appendix 3.1, at the back of this manual, gives a list of questions commonly asked by parents. We have provided suggested answers to these questions for you in preparation for the meeting.

It is impossible to predict all the questions which might be asked. If you should be asked a question to which you don't know the answer, say that you will find out and get back to them. You might be able to find the answer elsewhere in this manual. Alternatively, you could refer them to one of the local organisations that were represented at the planning meeting.

6. Parental Feedback

Ask the parents for their opinions and ideas. You may want to set a time limit of 15 minutes so the meeting does not go on forever.

7. Ending the Meeting

When there are no more questions, thank people for coming.

Now turn to the next chapter in this manual: After the Meeting. This explains what you need to do when the meeting is over and how to deal with situations that may arise some days after the meeting has taken place.

Chapter Three – After the Meeting

This chapter deals with requests from parents for further
information after the meeting.
It is divided into two sections:

1. Further Questions
2. Disclosure

1. Further Questions

The meeting usually provides the parents with all the
information needed. Some of the parents who attended the
meeting, however, may think of issues that need clarifying, or
questions that need answering, some time after the meeting has
finished. Some parents might have felt unsure about speaking in
a large group. For others, the meeting may have brought up
personal concerns and they may need further reassurance.

Hopefully, we will have anticipated most of the questions that
you are likely to be asked. These are given in Appendix 3.1 at
the back of this manual. If you are confronted by a request that
you can't meet, don't bluff! Either contact one of the local
agencies that are involved with the programme, or suggest that
the parent contact them direct.

Overload!

How you deal with parents after the meeting depends on how
much time you can afford. It is important that you don't create
problems for yourself by responding to more demands that you
can cope with.

To avoid being overloaded, make full use of the network of
local agencies and people that are involved with the programme.

2. Disclosure

Having presented the issues raised at the meeting, it is possible
that some parents will recall past experiences from their own
childhood during general conversation with you after the meeting
has ended. It is often these experiences which will lead to a very
positive and supportive reaction from parents to the programme.

You might find that a parent may be seeking an exclusive or
private opportunity to talk to you. This may be because:

— they suspect or know that their (or another) child is being
  abused
— they themselves were abused in childhood

If you receive any confirmation that either of these circumstances
is likely, first consider whether it is the most appropriate time
and place for dealing with the situation. You may need to
arrange another opportunity to continue the discussion.

Below are guidelines for dealing with either of these eventualities.

Suspicion or Knowledge of Child Abuse

- tell them that you cannot promise to keep what they tell you a secret if it involves the safety of children
- explain the procedure that the school has agreed for dealing with such incidents
- make sure that they understand to whom you will pass on the information that they give you
- ask them if they still want to tell you
- if they do tell you, believe what they say
- ask them if they want to contact the authority to which the school has decided to relay such information
- if they do, ask them if they would like your help to do this
- if they don't, tell them that you will contact the authority on their behalf, or on behalf of the child

Disclosure of Past Experience

- ask them if the offender is still likely to be abusing children
- if the answer is yes, go through the steps outlined above
- let them know that you understand how difficult it is to talk about such matters
- encourage them to speak, but try not to make judgements about what they are telling you
- ask them if they want to talk to someone who has experience of counselling victims of sexual assault
- if they do, recommend the person or organisation that you have identified during the Planning Meeting

Although you are not expected to be a therapist, just listening to someone who wants to tell you of a personal experience may be enormously helpful to them. In fact, that is all most people want to do. Many survivors of child abuse have related that being believed and supported by the first person they told was very important.

Before you begin to organise your parents' meetings, you will need to study Unit 4 of this manual: The Lesson. Turn to Unit 4.

Appendix 3.1 – Common Adult Concerns

Does talking about prevention frighten children?

We already warn children from an early age about the danger of going with strangers, but have seldom given them the kind of information they need to keep themselves safe, especially from abuse by people known to them. Ask any group of children about the kind of messages they have received and they will tell you of their fears.

Giving children ways to help prevent abuse makes them more aware and safe. It is a great relief to children that they are not being given yet more scare tactics and 'don'ts'. Good sense defence gives positive ideas and children enjoy learning how to stay safe. Children who know preventative techniques are not only less at risk because they are informed, but they are also more confident about themselves.

Will children lose trust in all adults if they are taught to say 'No' to people they know?

Children are only taught to say 'No' to touches, hugs or kisses that confuse or frighten them, or ones that are asked to be kept secret. There is never any reason to ask children to keep touching secret. Learning that they can say 'No' and get help if someone forces or tricks them into furtive touching does not affect their trust in adults, unless the adult is betraying that trust.

Won't children begin to refuse all kinds of affection?

Children are naturally affectionate, but should be allowed to choose to whom they will give their affection. If someone is making a child confused or uncomfortable with unwanted touching, hugging or kissing, then the child should have the right to say 'No' and get support to do this. Learning about good sense defence does not make children less affectionate, and it often makes them more comfortable about their own bodies.

Won't teaching children to say 'No' make them disobedient?

Children are taught to say 'No' only to uncomfortable or confusing touching. This is certainly not a licence for unruly children!

Isn't it better to say nothing or just concentrate on warnings about strangers?

Children have been left vulnerable for generations by lack of knowledge or warnings only about strangers. Since 75% of child sexual abuse is from someone the child knows, this warning is not enough. It is like teaching them to cross the road and only to watch for the red cars. According to the MORI survey, potentially 1 in 10 children will be subjected to a sexually abusive experience before the age of 16, so saying nothing is certainly not an effective method of protection.

Isn't it optimistic to think that children can always be kept safe?

Of course it would be unrealistic to think that. Unfortunately, there will always be circumstances in which children and adults will be harmed or even killed by determined attackers. But children can be taught with the help of their parents and teachers to think about how to keep themselves safe and to act to do so.

As it is, we do not give children enough information so that they can think for themselves. We teach children to always do exactly what any adult says. If an adult tells a child to get in a car, or touches them inappropriately, children often obey without question. Even if they feel instinctively that they should not. The message that good sense defence gives is that children can do anything necessary to stay safe, including breaking rules and that we as adults will support them. What we are trying to do is to minimise children's vulnerability.

Isn't there a danger that trying to resist might make the situation worse?

It is not possible to foresee what could happen in every circumstance. Once a child is in a dangerous situation, it is difficult to predict the outcome. That is why it is important to alert children to the potential dangers before it is too late to do anything. For example, yelling to attract attention, when getting help is still possible, makes sense. How would anyone know that a child needs help if the child does not somehow attract attention?

Teaching children to trust their feelings, and to recognise and anticipate dangers, encourages them to protect themselves before the situation gets out of control.

What about violence from the adult known to the child?

It is more unlikely that an adult known to the child will physically harm the child because the child said 'No'. However, children are given several strategies, including telling after the event, if that should prove necessary.

Does all this mean I have to be afraid to touch children?

Good hugs, kisses and touches teach children better than any other way the difference between furtive, forced or tricked touches and normal, everyday affection. However, adults should always be aware that sometimes children (and adults) do not want to be touched. For example, many children report that they hate being patted on the head or tickled.

No child should ever be forced to be affectionate with anyone, even parents or relatives. This gives the child conflicting messages about being able to say 'No'. 'Kiss Aunty goodbye – go on, silly! Do it!' How often do we force children into situations because we are embarrassed? Then what happens when a molester comes along and says, 'don't be so silly – do it!'

Aren't children sometimes provocative and therefore responsible for what happens?

Children are affectionate and seek adult attention. They are not seeking to be sexually abused. Children can be sensual, but it is the adult who puts a sexual connotation on the behaviour. However, sometimes children who have been abused will turn to adults in a sexual way because that is the only way the child has been taught to gain affection. In any case, it is up to the adult to act in a responsible way to protect and not to exploit the child. This includes children up to the age of 16.

What are the long-term effects of child sexual abuse?

It can lead to alcoholism, drugs, mental illness, prostitution, suicide attempts and abuse of future generations. It often produces feelings of guilt, anger and self-hatred. The effects are still being uncovered.

Are handicapped children at risk?

All children are at risk and should be taught good sense defence to the best of their ability to understand. The techniques of saying 'No' and getting help can be understood by most children.

Do all children who are abused grow up to abuse their own or other children?

No, there are many adults who, having experienced sexual, physical or emotional abuse as children, become loving parents and would never harm a child.

Won't talking about keeping safe make children who are already being abused feel worse?

Children who have been victims are usually relieved to find out that they are not the only ones that this has happened to. It gives them options which they might not have known about, particularly the option to tell. It does not mean that they will necessarily tell immediately, but they will know that it is possible. Often they must find the right time to tell.

What about children playing in a sexual way with themselves or other children?

Some children do experiment sexually with themselves and with other children. This should generally not be cause for concern. If, however, a child is trying to get other children to act in sexually explicit ways which are beyond the typical knowledge of a child of that age, this should be investigated.

What is a 'significant age' gap between children in terms of playing doctor or experimenting sexually?

This is not easily agreed upon as children mature at different levels. However, generally for children between the ages of 5 and 11, three years difference is significant. For teenagers, five years difference is considered by some experts to be significant.

Do children lie about sexual abuse? We know that they have active imaginations.

Children rarely lie about being sexually abused. They do not have the language or experience to describe this kind of abuse. Children may later retract an accusation of sexual abuse for fear of the consequences of having told or to protect someone. Also, because of the traumatic nature of events, details might be confused. In some cases of incestuous abuse, a child has accused someone other than the offender because he or she is too frightened to name the family member. This usually becomes obvious to an expert dealing with the child. However, the fact that the abuse occurred is true.

Very occasionally a child can be coached by an adult into saying abuse has occurred, for example in a divorce case. If this ever does happen, the child has not made it up, rather he or she has been forced or tricked by an adult. This is abusive to the child.

There have been several studies about false accusations of sexual abuse. In *The Journal of Interpersonal Violence*, March 1987, David P. H. Jones and J. Melbourne McGraw reported on a sample of 576 allegations of sexual abuse. They found a false reporting rate from adults and children of 8%. In the same article they mention studies by Goodwin, et al, 1982, which found 7% false reporting; Peters, 1976, found 6% false reporting; Horowitz, 1985, 5% false reporting. Some of the cases in the Jones study were children involved in custody disputes.

This indicates that the vast majority (92% to 95%) of reports of sexual abuse from people of *all* ages are not false allegations.

Why all the sudden interest in child sexual abuse? Is it on the increase?

Child sexual abuse has only recently been discussed in public, therefore we do not know if it is increasing. We know it has been going on since earliest times, but we are only now addressing the issues. There are some theories that the breakdown in families, unemployment, stress in modern life, child pornography and communication between offenders to rationalise their behaviour, has led to an increase. We do not know all the answers, but the increased awareness and public discussion is beginning to lead to a better understanding of the problem.

If it happens so much, why all the fuss? Maybe it's normal.

We are only now discovering the long-term effects on the victims of child sexual abuse. Child sexual abuse is not 'normal'. It is a crime against children.

Lock up the offenders!

It is often suggested that longer sentences for offenders would solve the problem of child sexual abuse. It is true that some offenders will always be a danger to children and should therefore have long sentences, which will keep children safe from them.

There are, however, offenders who are motivated to change their behaviour and who may benefit from treatment. In some of these cases, prison may be counter-productive. Alternatively, the threat or reality of a prison sentence can help to motivate the offender to change.

The real difficulty is that we are still learning how to treat the offenders. Research currently going on in Britain and other countries should lead to a greater understanding of these issues and how to deal with them.

Should adults talk to unaccompanied children?

Although most adults know that they are not strangers intent on harming children, children do not know that. If we teach children not to talk to people they do not know and then we ask children for directions or just chat to them, we do children a disservice. How are they to know that we mean them no harm? Most well-meaning adults do not approach children who are on their own and start a conversation with them. Obviously, if a child is in distress and needs assistance, this is a different matter.

I don't want my child involved.

Your answer to this will depend upon your school policy. You can say to the parent that if possible we will make alternative arrangements, but be sure to work out your answer and school policy before the meeting.

I would like my child to discuss the bullying, crime, etc., but not abuse (or some other lesson).

If the school is having separate lessons on each section, this is not difficult. However, if it is only one lesson, work out whatever you feel best for the child.

Shouldn't this be a subject that parents deal with at home?

Yes, and at school and in the community as a whole. Effectively teaching children good sense defence should be a co-operative undertaking with parents, teachers, and all other members of the community. No one individual or group can be expected to do it alone.

Appendix 3.2 – Letter to Parents

Dear Parent

We are planning to involve our students in the Kidscape programme *Teenscape*.

Hundreds of thousands of children, parents and teachers have taken part in the *Kidscape* programmes which have been designed to teach practical positive ways to help them stay safe.

Teenagers are taught to develop strategies to keep safe while out and about, to tell if they have a problem, what to do if bullied or if someone they know tries to abuse them in any way. The enclosed leaflets list the lessons and some of the background about the programme, and also give facts, danger signs and advice about what to do if a child tells about abuse.

The success of the programme depends upon parents, teachers and other concerned adults being supportive and helping teenagers to use common sense in keeping safe.

Knowing that you may want to hear more about the issues such as sexual abuse, and discuss your ideas and concerns, we have arranged a meeting on

_____ at_____ p.m.

in the _____

So we can plan for the meeting, we would greatly appreciate your detaching and returning the slip below.

We look forward to seeing you.

Yours sincerely

– –

I will/will not be able to attend the meeting for parents

Name _____

Name(s) of Child(ren) _____

Signature _____

Appendix 3.3 – Kidscape Leaflet, A Programme for Your Child's Protection

KIDSCAPE 'Good Sense Defence' programmes have been developed to help children and young people become better able to recognise and cope with a variety of potentially dangerous situations, from bullying to approaches from known adults who might attempt to harm them.

The KIDSCAPE programmes were written by Michele Elliott, teacher, psychologist and mother of two. Michele has chaired Home Office and World Health Organisation Working Groups on the Prevention of Child Abuse. She has over 20 years of experience in this field.

'Good Sense Defence' for the Young

Hundreds of thousands of children, parents and teachers have taken part in the KIDSCAPE programmes. The approach is low-key, matter-of-fact and non-sensational.

Although the strategies are taught to children, the success of the programme depends upon and involves parents, teachers, youth workers, police and all other concerned adults.

The Kidscape Keepsafe Code

Teenscape helps young people develop strategies without frightening them.

In the lessons young people learn about:

- Trusting Intuition – getting away if a situation seems 'not right'
- Saying 'No' – it is not always easy to say 'No' when friends ask you to do something or if you are frightened
- Safety When Out – 'What If' you are being followed or you need to make an emergency telephone call
- Bullying – why does it happen, what can you do, should there be 'bully arbitration courts' run by students
- Crime – what is serious, what are student attitudes, how would you deal with crime/punishment
- Abuse – what is abuse, who is affected, what are your concerns about the laws, your feelings, the abusers
- Keeping Safe from Abuse – telling, getting help, it's not your fault if it has happened
- Common Sense Defence – creating a fuss, kicking, getting away if you are attacked
- Addiction/Gambling – why do people become addicted, what are they looking for

Available from Kidscape

For Parents:
- *Keeping Safe, a practical guide to talking with children* by Michele Elliott. Gives ways of talking to children about keeping safe.

For Children:
- *The Willow Street Kids, It's Your Right to be Safe* by Michele Elliott. Written for junior age children, it answers children's questions and will help them to learn to keep safe in a variety of situations.

For Teachers and Trainers:
- The Kidscape Kits – *The Primary Kit, Under Fives Manual, Teenscape*, all for use in schools.
- Kidscape Training Guide – Provides in-depth training in prevention of child sexual abuse.

——————————————————————————————

For a full list of materials and services available from Kidscape, write to:

KIDSCAPE (Information)
World Trade Centre
Europe House
London E1 9AA

Name ....

Address ....

....
(In Capitals Please)

Comments about the Kidscape Approach

What parents say . . .

I was most impressed and found it very reassuring. It gave me a language to talk with my children about keeping safe.
Mr. Mitchell

My children enjoyed it because it was fun to do. They heard what was said and took it in. They didn't associate it with sex, but rather with taking care of themselves. Thank you for such a positive programme.

Mrs Harris

What teachers say . . .

The workshops with the children are fantastic. The programme has made it easy to teach personal safety without making children uncomfortable or frightened.
Fiona Crampton, Class Teacher

The most comprehensive programme I have ever seen. It created a real bond of trust and empathy between teachers and pupils. Parents said how pleased they were at how the subject was handled.

Linda Frost, Head Teacher

The approach makes teaching the subject just another part of child safety in the same way that we take children to see fire engines for fire safety.

Jim Norwood, Headmaster

What children say . . .

I learned that you should tell your mum and dad if anyone asked you to keep kisses a secret and don't go into people's cars that you don't know.

Stephen

About three weeks after the lesson someone tried to get me into his car. I stayed far away and ran into a shop.

Sharon

What the press say . . .

'Good Sense Defence is a slogan that could soon be on the lips of most children in this country'

Sunday Times, January 1986

Childhood Should be . . .

A time of joy and discovery in which children are nurtured and loved, so that they may grow into caring adults. Part of the process of discovery and growth must also help children to learn how to cope with potential dangers.

We teach children road and water safety so that they can cross the road, and go near and into the water without being harmed. We do not find this particularly difficult because these are accepted as risks. Neglecting this advice would be considered foolish by most adults.

Children are also warned of the dangers of talking to or going with strangers, not because the vast marjority of adults would harm children, but because of the few deviant individuals who might. Ask any children over the age of three and they will tell you 'never take sweets from a stranger'. But have we done our duty to children by only warning them about stranger danger?

In 75% of the reported cases of child sexual assault in Britain, the offender was known by the child. Therefore, just warning children about strangers is like teaching them to cross the road watching only for red cars.

Although it is not possible to eliminate completely the causes of child assault, it is possible to reduce the vulnerability of children by giving them information which will help keep them safe. Kidscape call this Good Sense Defence.

KIDSCAPE

World Trade Centre,
Europe House,
London E1 9AA

**Appendix 3.4 –
Kidscape Leaflet
Child Sexual Abuse**
The Facts

Child sexual abuse is the exploitation of a child under the age of 16 for the sexual gratification of an older person. Sexual abuse of children is not new; what is new is public concern and the willingness to discuss this emotive issue.

- A MORI survey estimated that 1 in 10 British adults had at least one sexually abusive experience in childhood, ranging from obscene telephone calls, to fondling and rape
- 75% of the reported cases in Britain of child sexual abuse were committed by someone known to the child
- Girls and boys are both at risk
- The vast majority of reported offenders are male, most victims of child abuse themselves
- Children are not responsible for being sexually abused
- Children rarely lie about sexual abuse, though they may deny it happened out of fear or to protect someone
- Sexual abuse of children occurs in every class and race
- Child sexual abuse can cause mistrust and guilt, and damage a child's self-image
- Lack of information makes children vulnerable

Danger Signs

Although these signs do not necessarily indicate that a child has been sexually abused, they may help adults recognise that something is wrong. The possibility of sexual abuse should be investigated if a child shows a number of these symptoms, or any one of them to a marked degree:

- Personality changes such as becoming insecure or clinging
- Regressing to younger behaviour patterns such as thumb sucking or bringing out discarded cuddly toys
- Sudden loss of appetite or compulsive eating
- Being isolated or withdrawn
- Inability to concentrate
- Lack of trust in an adult that they know well, such as not wanting to be alone with a babysitter or child minder
- Starting to wet again, day or night.
  Nightmares, being unable to sleep
- Being overly affectionate or knowledgeable in a sexual way inappropriate to the child's age
- Medical problems such as chronic itching, pain in the genitals, venereal diseases
- Other extreme reactions, such as depression, self-mutilation, suicide attempts, running away, overdoses, anorexia
- It is also possible that a child may show no outward signs and hide what is happening from everyone

If a Child Tells you:

- Stay calm and be reassuring
- Find a quiet place to talk
- Believe what you are being told
- Listen, but do not press for information
- Say that you are glad that the child told you
- If it will help the child to cope, say that the offender has a problem
- Say that you will do your best to protect and support the child
- If necessary, seek medical help and contact the police or social services
- If your child has told another adult, such as a teacher or school nurse, contact them. Their advice may make it easier to help your child
- Determine if this incident may affect how your child reacts at school. It may be advisable to liaise with your child's teacher, school nurse or headteacher
- Acknowledge that your child may have angry, sad or even guilty feelings about what happened, but stress that the abuse was not the child's fault. Acknowledge that you will probably need help dealing with your own feelings
- Seek counselling for yourself and your child through the organisations listed or through your own contacts

Kidscape 'Good Sense Defence'

Based on a two year pilot project involving thousands of parents, children and teachers in schools in Britain, KIDSCAPE has developed a concept called 'Good Sense Defence'. It teachers children positive, practical ways to help keep them safe from various dangers, including sexual abuse.

'Good Sense Defence' is child-centred, but its success depends upon everyone within the community who cares for children being actively involved.

The pilot project was so successful and the demand so great that the technique has now been designed as a programme in kit form so that it is available to any school which wants to use it. Training courses are also available for professionals.

Available from KIDSCAPE:

For schools:
The Kidscape Primary Kit, the *Under Fives Manual*, *Teenscape*
For adults:
Keeping Safe, a practical guide to talking with children by Michele Elliott
For children:
The Willow Street Kids, It's Your Right to be Safe by Michele Elliott

For more details about the above, contact:
KIDSCAPE
World Trade Centre
Europe House
London E1 9AA.

Where to Get Help

You may consider using the school as a resource, as the staff should have a network of agencies they work with, and will be able to give you advice

You can contact official agencies or self-help groups. If you are concerned about what action may be taken, ask before you proceed

The following can be contacted through your telephone directory:

- Police
- Social Services
- National Society for the Prevention of Cruelty to Children (NSPCC) in England, Wales and Northern Ireland
- Royal Scottish Society for the Prevention of Cruelty to Children (RSSPCC)
- Irish Society for the Prevention of Cruelty to Children (ISPCC)
- Telephone counselling services:
  Childline 0800 1111
  Mothers of Abused Children:
  Located in Cumbria – 0965 31432
  Rape Crisis Centres:
  See local directory or ring 01-837 1600
- Organisations which help parents under stress:
  Parents Anonymous, 6pm to 6am 01-263 8918
  Organisations for Parents Under Stress 0602 819 423
  Family Network 01-514 1177;
  Scotland (041) 221 6722;
  Wales (0222) 29461

KIDSCAPE, World Trade Centre, Europe House,
London E1 9AA
Telephone: 071-488 0488

Both of these KIDSCAPE leaflets are also available in Urdu, Hindi, Bengali, Gujarati, Punjabi, Cantonese, Greek and Turkish.

Unit 4 — Lessons for Teenscape

1. Introduction

There are two issues in this introductory lesson. The first is to set up groundrules and contracts which will guide all of the work done with students in the *Teenscape* lessons. The second is to begin to address the feelings the students may have when discussing emotive subjects like abuse or bullying.

It is important that the issue of groundrules be sorted out first to ensure that the students feel comfortable and safe when sharing feelings. Depending upon the amount of time available, you may wish to divide the lesson into two parts and teach it on different days.

As with all the lessons, we provide a script, realising that you may use it as is or change it to suit your teaching style and the ability of your students.

Groundrules/Contracts

'During this term, we are going to be exploring the issues around personal safety and how to say 'No' and get help in difficult situations. These situations can cover a wide range of topics, such as bullying, crime, physical, emotional or sexual abuse and perhaps some ideas on self-defence.

Some of the things we talk about could be embarrassing or painful or cause you to laugh. The lessons will involve some role-playing, stories, and discussions with many of the ideas coming from you. So I would like to ask your help setting up some groundrules for all of our lessons and discussions about personal safety. When we have a list of groundrules, we will discuss them and then agree on which ones we will follow as a class. This will be our class contract.'

If you have confidence that you can discuss any topic of interest to students (and the governors wouldn't object) you could also have the students brainstorm topics which would be of interest to them. But do not give them the opportunity to do this unless there is a chance to follow through or it will be a pointless exercise. You could also give them the topics listed for the lessons and ask them to tell you of their particular interests or concerns or have them break the topics into sub-groups.

'We are going to break up into small groups in a moment to brainstorm, but perhaps it would be helpful if I gave you one or two examples of groundrules.

Let's say we are discussing the problem of bullying and there is someone in the class who is either a bully or a victim. I would like to see a groundrule which says that we will not name people nor make jokes at anyone's expense, and if there is laughter it will not be directed towards someone else.'

This might translate into two groundrules.

WRITE ON THE BOARD:
GROUNDRULES

1. Not to embarrass others
2. Not to make fun of anyone

Decide how you are going to divide the class (i.e. groups of six, eight, mixed groups of boys and girls, single sex, self-selecting, etc.).

'Would you now get into your groups and ask one person to be your scribe or secretary. That person will write the group's ideas on this large piece of paper in big letters.

After you have thought of and written down your ideas for groundrules, we will put up the sheets of paper so that everyone can see what each group has written. You will have five minutes, so think fast and put down as many ideas as you can during that time.'

Give each group a large piece of paper and a felt-tip marker.

It may be that your students will need longer or shorter time to brainstorm. When the students have completed the groundrules sheets, bring them together as a large group and have each group put up their ideas.

As the groups share their ideas for groundrules, write them on the board (or have a student do this) without comment. It usually works better if you take one idea from each group and then go around again. Otherwise, one group may give all the ideas and the other groups will get bored or restless.

When you have recorded the groundrules, decide which ones are agreeable to everyone. One class listed the following groundrules:

— Not to embarrass others
— Not to make fun of anyone
— Allow time to talk
— No put-downs
— What is said in the lessons is confidential
— To be supportive of others
— No-one is allowed to talk for more than two minutes at a time
— No-one to act like a jerk
— No violence
— Class votes on who to invite in to speak
— Teacher willing to talk privately to students, but not able to promise confidentiality if s/he thinks the student is at risk

This last groundrule was suggested by the teacher, who in this case was willing to spend the extra time. You will need to decide that for yourself.

When the groundrules are agreed, have someone make a poster-type list which is posted. This is the class contract. The contract will be helpful in deciding what to do about bullying. In fact, you may find these groundrules useful for all lessons, not just *Teenscape*.

You may want to agree a plan in case someone breaks the contract. What consequences will follow? One class decided that anyone who broke the rules would be made to write up ideas about the lesson and present them to the class. You may decide to exclude someone from a lesson, but there is always the possibility that the student is reacting because the issue hits too close to home.

Feelings

The second task is to deal with the feelings which may arise from discussing emotive and embarrassing issues. We suggest that you ask the students to go back into their groups and make another list of possible feelings which may arise while talking about the *Teenscape* lessons. Provide them with a list of the topics in the lessons (either on the board or on handouts).

Ask that they again appoint a scribe and come up with a list in five minutes.

'We are now going back into the same groups to brainstorm about the types of feelings which may come up when discussing some of these topics. For example, when talking about bullying, some people may feel angry, others may feel scared. When discussing other subjects such as Safety When Out, if you have had the experience of being mugged or beaten up, you may feel sad, miserable, furious, powerless, etc. So there are many different ways of reacting to these issues.'

Write down some of the possible feelings on the board to give the students a model. Have them go back into their groups and give them five minutes to brainstorm.

Allow more time if the exercise is bringing out productive discussion. When they have finished, again make a list of possible feelings, taking one or two initially from each group. The list might read:

— Angry
— Hurt
— Fearful
— Happy
— Sad
— Disgusted
— Mean
— Furious

It is important to make a collective list so that the students will know that it is alright to have these feelings and that it is normal. It sets the tone for the work to follow in the other lessons.

'There are feelings that many people have when talking about some of these situations. Some people react differently to the same situations. For example, one person might be furious if his or her little brother was beaten up and another might feel happy. It will be important as we talk about personal safety and all the issues to recognise your feelings and talk with someone about them. You may want to think of who you could talk to, like a gran or mum or dad, a friend, a teacher, etc.'

Here you must again decide if you want to be available for the students for private or small group talks. Students will choose their confidants, but sometime it is comforting to know that a teacher or youth worker or another adult has made the offer of listening (without promises of confidentiality).

The list of feelings is not necessarily to be posted. The purpose is to bring the idea of expressing them into the open. You may wish to continue the discussion by having the students think of acceptable ways to express feelings. When going through the lessons, there will be opportunities to turn feelings into positive steps. For example, if students are angry about bullying, there are ways to come to grips with the problem by turning the anger into action like setting up bullying arbitration courts.

'In our next session we will be talking about feeling safe and how our intuition or instincts might help us to keep safe.'

2. Trusting Intuition

'Often the ability to keep safe depends upon trusting those feelings which we call intuition. Can you give me an example of trusting your intuition?'

If no-one has any suggestions, offer an example such as:

'Michael went out with some friends to the cinema. As Michael and his friends were walking home, a group of older boys came towards them. Even from a distance, Michael could see they were drunk and looking for trouble. He had the feeling that if he and his friends didn't do something, there was going to be a fight. If he trusted that intuitive feeling, what do you think he should do?'

Have the class brainstorm answers and write them on the board without comment. Have the class divide into discussion groups to decide which of the answers they think would work in a real-life situation. Bring the class back together when they have had sufficient time and agree on strategies which might work. These may include:

— Crossing over the road
— Going into a cafe or some other place to get off the street
— Going back to the cinema

One way to help teenagers to think about strategies is to get them to dramatise the situations. Having determined some possible strategies to keep safe and trust their intuition, ask the students to roleplay. If you have three possible solutions, you may want to add another way to deal with the problem, such as confrontation.

Remind the class of the groundrules. If a groundrule was not made about physical violence, bring the issue to the attention of the students and agree to no actual physical violence during the dramatisation. It is possible, that students will roleplay situations which involve violent situations to problems. If this happens, allow time for discussion to explore what would happen if a violent course of action was employed and the possible consequences.

Divide the students into four groups, give them ten minutes to produce a two-minute roleplay. Have each group present to the class and discuss.

Another method is general class discussion. Ask the class if any of them have ever been in a situation in which they followed their intuition to stay safe. Depending upon the students, you could also ask if there was a time when they didn't follow their feelings, and ask what about the resulting consequences. There is a danger that a child could get upset when relaying such a story or even that a disclosure of abuse could result, so use this question with caution.

Follow-up activities

• Write fictional stories
• Write about personal experiences
• Conduct a survey asking other students about situations in which they have trusted their intuition to help themselves. Ensure that identity of those answering the survey is

anonymous. Ask only for positive examples to avoid embarrassment. There could be an optional question about times when students did not follow their intuition and the consequences, but this would have to be handled with care. A sample questionnaire might read:

Have you ever been in a situation in which you listened to your own intuition to get away or keep safe?

_____ YES   _____NO

If yes, could you briefly describe the incident?

_____

_____

_____

_____

What do you think might have happened if you had not trusted your intuition?

_____

_____

_____

Optional question

Have you ever been in a situation which your instincts told you was wrong or dangerous and you did not follow your instincts to get away or get help?

_____YES   _____NO

If yes, can you explain what happend?

_____

_____

_____

How might it have been different if you had followed your intuition?

_____

_____

_____

Compile the results of the questionnaire/survey and publish it for students' use. This type of exercise may help teenagers to think carefully about following their intuition should they ever be in a difficult situation. Stories from peers often make a bigger impact than a lecture from an adult.

3. Saying 'No'

Ask the students:

'Do you sometimes find it difficult to say 'No'? Perhaps you can think of a time when it was difficult to say 'No', even though you wanted to. It could be any time in your life. For example, when you were younger, did you ever have to kiss someone goodbye at the end of a visit? Or did you have to stop watching a favourite television programme in the middle because dinner was ready? Or did you have to say 'yes please' to some food you didn't really want?'

Either carrying on with a class discussion or divide the students into small groups. Ask:

'Can anyone think of a particular incident when they wanted to say 'No', but couldn't?'

'How did you feel?'

If the students are in small groups, ask them to choose one of the shared experiences and roleplay it, but they must do it without words. Present the roleplays to the class and see if the rest of the students can understand the situation.

Discuss the body language of not being able to say 'No' – dropped shoulders, unhappy faces, fear, etc.

Then have the groups talk about how it would have been different if they could have said 'No'. Roleplay the same situations with the child or teenagers being empowered to say 'No', again without words.

Discuss the differences. If you choose to have a class discussion instead of a roleplay, ask for positive experiences and compare the difference in feelings between the situations.

Activities

Ask the students to divide into pairs. Have one walk like a victim or someone who cannot say 'No'. Have the other follow the 'victim', but act assertively and walk confidently. Stop the activity after a minute and have them reverse roles.

Discuss the difference in feelings of walking and acting like a 'victim' and walking confidently.

'If you were looking for a victim, which person would you approach?'

Ask the students to pretend that they dislike cooked carrot and turnip pie. (Or ask the students to suggest something.) Tell them that you are going to feed them this for lunch, unless they can convince you that they don't really want it. Ask them to say 'No' as a group, in response to your statement 'I am giving you a

delicious cooked carrot and turnip pie for lunch'. If the first 'no' is not assertive enough, have them stand up and shout 'No', using appropriate body language. Be sure to warn your neighbouring teachers!

Ensure that the students yell 'No' from the stomach, not from the throat. Have them take a deep breath and feel the yell come from the stomach.

As a follow-up, ask the students when they think it might be appropriate to yell 'No' and when it might be better to remain silent. For example:

> What if you were in an isolated place with a person who had a weapon and he said 'I'll kill you if you scream'?

Have the students come up with 'what if' type situations so they can begin to anticipate what strategies they might use.

4. Feeling Safe

There are several ways this session can begin. One way would be to ask the students in a large group discussion when and where they feel safe. Another would be to have them break into discussion groups as in Session 1 and have them come up with a list. Perhaps the most active and engaging way would be to have the students divide into groups of six and come up with ideas about feeling safe and then have them roleplay one or more of their ideas to the whole group.

If you decide on a group discussion, the following are some possible questions to get the discussion started:

'When do you feel safe?'
'Where do you feel safe?'
'With whom do you feel safe?'
'Are there places, times or people with whom you do not feel safe?'

Activities

Depending upon the age of your students, you may want to extend this into making posters or writing stories or doing roleplays. It might be possible to have some students carry out a research project with other students or parents or teachers/staff about attitudes towards personal safety. A graph of responses could be posted in the school, such as:

Students in this school say they feel safe:

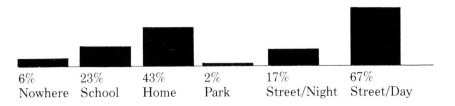

| 6% | 23% | 43% | 2% | 17% | 67% |
| Nowhere | School | Home | Park | Street/Night | Street/Day |

Points to stress
Everyone has the right to be safe – children, youths, parents,
teachers, police, old people.
No-one should take away that right.

5. Safety When Out

Start by asking the teenagers what their concerns are for their
own safety. Have them work in groups to come up with a list,
which you can then write on the board without comment.

Ask them how many of them have ever experienced an attack
or been mugged or threatened. The results of this are often
surprising. In one group of 110 fourteen-year-olds, thirty-one had
been physically attacked or mugged. Twenty-nine had never told
their parents and the majority were boys. They did not tell their
parents for fear that the parents would not let them out again.

If there is time, have the students make up a questionnaire for
the rest of the student body to see the extent of their
experiences. We are talking about stranger or acquaintance
attacks here.

Have the students break into groups to discuss the 'What If'
situations listed below. Ask each group to present three or four
ideas to the rest of the group. Students can also roleplay the
situations.

If the students are reluctant to admit that they are at risk, ask
them to say what advice they would give to a younger child, such
as a brother or sister. (Be prepared for wisecracks!)
What if . . .

1. You were walking down the street alone and you thought you
   were being followed.

   a) It is daytime and you can see people in the distance.
   b) It is late at night and no-one is around.

2. You were approached by someone demanding money:

   a) on a busy high street
   b) in a lonely back street
   c) the person has a knife or another weapon

3. Someone actually grabbed you and tried to pull you into a
   car or towards deserted grounds.

4. You are home alone and a delivery person comes to the door
   with flowers, groceries, a package, etc. You are not expecting
   anyone.

5. A man comes to the door saying his car has broken down
   and his wife is having a baby. Can he phone for an
   ambulance?

6. You are travelling on a bus/train/underground alone and:

   a) someone flashes at you
   b) someone starts touching you
   c) someone whispers obscenities at you
   d) someone seems to be following you when you leave

e) someone starts hitting you

7. You need to make an emergency telephone call, but you have no money.
8. You are at a party. There are no adults in the house/flat. A gang of kids gate-crashes the party. The boy giving the party has not told his parents about the party and begs you not to call the police or his parents will kill him.
9. You are jogging in the park with your Walkman on. Someone pulls you to the ground and starts attacking you.
10. You miss the last bus home after a party . . .
11. You come into your block of flats and a person you have never seen before comes up behind you and waits for you to open the door.
12. You are getting into the lift alone and someone you vaguely know gets in, but makes you feel very uncomfortable.
13. You are babysitting and the person who is supposed to take you home is drunk.
14. You are in a public toilet and the person next to you tries to touch you.
15. You come home alone and hear or see what appears to be a burglary going on in your flat/house.

Follow-up activities

Divide the students into groups again and ask them to devise a 'What If' questionnaire for the rest of the class/school. Have them administer the questionnaire and publish the results.

6. Bullying

'Bullying has been a problem for many people, both the victims and the bullies. I would like to find out what you think about the problem and how you think it can be solved. If it is not a problem for you or anyone you know, then perhaps you can think of what can be done for either younger children or for other people.'

Divide the class into small groups, if possible, or have a large class discussion. Some of the issues and concerns can be raised with the following questions:

- Can you define bullying?
- What do you think the characteristics of bullies are?
- Why do people bully?
- Who are the victims?
- Does anyone deserve to be bullied?
- Is there a problem with bullying in this school/neighbourhood/ youth centre/etc.?
- If so, what can be done about it?

This kind of work will start students talking about and recognising the problem. Their ideas and suggestions can be presented to the class (from small groups) or written up from the class discussion.

Some suggestions:

Do a survey to find out about the problem by devising a simple questionnaire along the lines:

a) Do you consider that you have ever been bullied? Yes____ No____

b) At what age? ____ under five ____ 5–11 ____ 11–14 ____ Over 14

c) Did/do you consider the bullying to have been

  ____ no problem ____ worrying ____ frightening

  ____ so bad that you didn't want to go out or to school

d) Did the bullying

  ____ have no effect ____ some bad effect ____ terrible effect

  ____ make you change your life in some way (e.g. change schools or move out of a neighbourhood)

e) What do you think of bullies?

  ____ no feeling ____ feel sorry for them ____ hate them

  ____ like them

f) Who is responsible when bullying continues to go on?

  ____ the bully ____ the bully's parents ____ the teachers

  ____ the head ____ the victim ____ children who are not being bullied, but do not help the victim ____ others

g) Please tick if you are a girl ____ boy ____

h) Was the bully (bullies) a girl ____ boy ____

i) If you have ever been bullied, was the bullying

  physical ____ emotional ____ verbal ____
  (you may tick more than one)

j) Where did the bullying happen?

  _____

  _____

  _____

k) What should be done about the problem of bullying?

  _____

  _____

  _____

l) Have you ever bullied anyone? ____Yes ____No

Possible Suggestions:

- 'Bully Arbitration Courts' run by students (see page 104).
- Meetings between bully and teacher/victim.

- Involving parents in meetings to address the problem and get their suggestions.
- The Code of Silence that teens keep – discuss making the school a 'telling school' in which it is the obligation of the students to tell.
- Have the students write roleplays about bullies and present them to the class or school.
- Have students design a leaflet (example on page 102).
- Break up gangs of bullies (see page 105).
- Call an assembly to discuss the problem of bullying schoolwide.
- Work out a school policy on bullying, involving students and teachers. Present the results to a parents' meeting and seek their support.
- Arrange for the bully to get counselling.
- Help the victims become more assertive and self-confident. Discuss how to talk your way out of a fight and reinforce the message that your school does not support violence. Students could roleplay when it is wise to walk away from a situation:

  The bully is becoming physically abusive and is beginning to come towards you. What do you do?

- Have the students roleplay several situations and discuss them, deciding upon which strategies might work. Is it wise to go on the offensive in some situations? Is it ever a good idea to just remain silent? Should you pour fuel on the fire by making the other person angrier?
- If bullying is going on, do you ever call in the authorities, i.e. the police? Under what circumstances?
- If a bully actually did physically attack you, what would you do? (See Common Sense Defence)
- Discuss the attitude of the students towards each other. Are they supportive? If someone is being bullied, do other students help, ignore or join in? What suggestions have the students for those who are not being bullied or those who are not the bullies?
- Discuss with staff the following 'Suggestions for Teachers' and decide what strategies the adults need to adopt to help eradicate bullying.
- See Appendix 4.1 for an example of how one teenage boy turned his experience of being bullied into a literary exercise: it might stimulate class discussion.

Suggestions for Teachers

1. Tell the children from day one that bullying (verbal or physical) is *not* tolerated in the school. Everyone is expected to ensure that it does not happen and has the responsibility to tell – this is not telling tales.
2. In class, have the children discuss bullying; what it is, what can be done, etc.

3. Have the children do a school survey to find out what children, teachers and staff think about bullying. Is it a problem, should it go on, should children tell if they are being bullied?
4. Have the children compile the survey and allow them to call a school assembly to announce the results.
5. Have the classes make up rules for behaviour. Agree a class/ school set of rules.
6. Agree possible solutions (or punishments if necessary). This can be done by the children in 'bullying courts'.
7. Have the children discuss ways to help the bullies become part of the group.
8. If bullying is going on, find out the facts, talk to the bullies and victims individually. If the bullying is about a particular issue (e.g. death, divorce, disfigurement), mount an education programme about the problem, but not focused on a particular child. Call in parents, ask their suggestions and solicit their support.
9. If necessary break up the group dynamics by assigning places, keeping bullies at school at the end of the day, etc. Most bullying groups have a leader with other children being frightened of *not* bullying. Turn peer pressure against bullying and break up groups.
10. Teach children to be assertive using programmes such as *Kidscape*. Differences should be acceptable and never a cause for bullying. Reward and encourage children for individuality.

Kidscape Bullying Leaflet

Bullying

BULLIES MAKE LIFE MISERABLE FOR MANY CHILDREN. SOME PEOPLE ARE BULLIES BECAUSE THEY ARE:

- Unhappy
- Insecure
- Bullied at home
- Not allowed to show feelings
- Cowards at heart
- Self hating

BULLIES APPEAR VERY POWERFUL. THEY MAY EVEN MAKE IT SEEM LIKE THE BULLYING IS THE VICTIM'S FAULT.

Help!

If bullying is chronic and severe, it is probably affecting many children. The behaviour must be stopped for the sake of the victims and the bullies.

SOME THINGS ADULTS SHOULD ABOUT BULLYING:

- Not allow it anywhere.
- Support children who are being bullied.
- Help the bullies to change their behaviour.
- Tell children to tell and back them up.
- Take bullying seriously and find out the facts when told about an incident of bullying.
- Inform parents if children are being bullied or if children are bullies at school.
- Meet with the bullies and victims individually.
- Ensure that children, parents and teachers take responsibility for any bullying that goes on to anyone.
- Set up discussion groups and lessons about bullying.
- Break up groups of bullies by not allowing them to play, sit, eat, etc, together.
- If bullying is happening to children on the way home, keep the bullies at school until everyone has left. Do not allow the bullies to leave together.
- Use peer pressure against bullying behaviour.
- Help children think about strategies to use.
- If necessary, help the children set up 'bullying courts' which decide how to deal with bullying. Roleplay situations.

SOME THINGS TO DO IF YOU ARE BEING BULLIED:

- Tell an adult you trust.
- Tell yourself that you don't deserve to be bullied.
- Get your friends together and say no to the bully.
- Stay with groups of people, even if they are not your friends. There is safety in numbers.
- Try to ignore the bullying.
- Try not to show you are upset, which is difficult.
- If possible, avoid being alone in places where bullying happens.
- Try being assertive – shout 'No' loudly. Practise in front of a mirror.
- Walk quickly and confidently even if you don't feel that way inside. Practise!
- If you are in danger, get away. Do not fight to keep possessions.
- Fighting back may make it worse. If you decide to fight back, talk to an adult first.
- If you are different in some way, be proud of it! It is good to be an individual.

Contact
- The teacher, headteacher, parent governors on your school's board; the education welfare officer or the educational psychologist; your MP; and finally the media.
- Citizen's Advice Bureaux (local directory)
- Children's Legal Centre 01-359 6251

Telephone Helplines
- Childline 0800 1111
- Samaritans (local directory)
- OPUS (Organisation for Parents Under Stress) 01-645 0469
- Family Network: Scotland 041-221 6722; Wales 0222 29461; North of England 061-236 9873; South of England 0582 422751
- Education Otherwise 01-904 7155 (Advice about home education)

Books

The Willow Street Kids, Michele Elliott, Pan/Piccolo (5–11 yrs)
Growing Pains and How to Avoid Them, Claire Rayner, Heinemann (Teens)
Too Close Encounters and What To Do About Them, Rosemary Stones, Piccadilly (Teens)
Keeping Safe, A Practical Guide to Talking With Children, Michele Elliott, Hodder & Stoughton (Parents/Teachers)
Bullies and Victims in Schools: A Guide to Understanding and Management, Valerie E. Besag, Open University Press (Teachers)

Videos for Teens

A Time To Live, Samaritans. Deals with subjects from bullying to suicide. Contact your local Samaritans branch for details.

Bully Courts

1. Agree guidelines for behaviour with students.
2. Sign individual contracts with each student re. guidelines.
3. Post the guidelines on bulletin boards throughout the school.
4. Call a school assembly and have students present guidlines; include all staff, including playground supervisors.
5. As part of the guidelines, set up an arbitration court to rule on infractions.
6. The court could comprise of four students, two elected by the student body and two appointed (as an honour) by the teachers.
7. One teacher would sit on the court (which could be called an Honour Court).
8. The term of office depends upon the agreement of the students – one school term would be suggested.
9. Unless there was an emergency, the court would meet once a week at a set time.
10. The court would be responsible for most infractions, unless they were serious enough to involve the police (i.e. assault) or there was a family problem which made it inappropriate.
11. Solutions and/or penalties would be binding on all parties, with the right of appeal. Possible penalties should be in keeping with school policy – a list would be helpful.

12. The verdict of the court would be written down and filed, with copies going to all concerned parties.
13. School governors and parents would all receive information about the court and be invited to a meeting to see a mock case and to discuss the issues.
14. The effectiveness of the court would be evaluated by students, parents and teachers.

Breaking Up Bully Gangs

1. Meet with victim or victims separately – have them write down what happened.
2. Meet with each member of the gang separately – have them write down what happened.
3. Agree with each member of the gang separately what you expect and discuss how s/he has broken the contract about guidelines for behaviour (see Bully Courts, points 1–4).
4. Meet with gang as a group and have each state what happened in your individual meeting; ensure that everyone is clear about what is expected.
5. Prepare them to face their peer group – 'What are you going to say when you leave here?'
6. Decide about involving the Bully Courts – this will depend upon what you have agreed with the students.
7. Whatever is decided, reiterate to all students that they are all responsible if anyone is being bullied – there are no innocent bystanders.
8. Talk to parents of all involved – show them written statements.
9. Keep a file on bullying with all statements and penalties.
10. Teach victims strategies (as in *Kidscape* lessons).
11. Do not accept false excuses:

    • If it (the bullying) was an accident, did the children act by helping the victim or getting help or giving sympathy?
    • If it was just for a laugh, was everyone laughing?
    • If it was a game, was everyone enjoying it?

12. If a child is injured, take photographs of the injury.
13. If gangs of bullies from outside your school appear, take photographs – they tend to run when they see the camera.
14. If there is serious injury, contact the police.

7. Crime

'Crime is something which affects us all. We are going to be discussing the problem of crime and how it affects you and others in the community.'

Have the students divide into groups of six with the task of defining what they think crime is. The following exercise may help them to get started:

Using this list, you are to agree which of the crimes you would label

- 'Extremely dangerous'
- 'Serious'
- 'Not serious'

You must all agree to the label you put next to the crime. You cannot put, for example, 'Serious/Not serious'. It must be one label only.

— Murder of an old lady
— Murder of an old man
— Murder of a child
— Murder of someone your age
— Murder of someone you love
— Rape of an old lady
— Rape of a child
— Rape of someone your age
— Mugging of an old person
— Mugging of a young woman
— Mugging with a weapon such as a knife
— Beating up an old person
— Beating up a child
— Beating up someone you love
— Beating up a person for racial reasons
— Having a bicycle stolen
— An old person having their pension stolen
— A mother stealing food from a shop to feed her children
— Shoplifting from a big department store
— Shoplifting from a small local shop
— A stranger stealing something from a shop
— A friend stealing something from a shop
— Getting drunk and smashing a window
— Getting drunk and beating someone up
— Making obscene comments to a stranger on the street
— Making an obscene telephone call to your home
— Flashing to a child
— Flashing to a person your age
— Dropping a rock from a bridge on to a motorway
— Throwing a rock at a train
— Stealing a car which belongs to a poor person
— Stealing a car which belongs to a wealthy person
— Running down a pedestrian and driving off
— Under-age drinking
— Drinking and driving
— Sniffing glue/other solvent
— Using marijuana
— Using cocaine
— Using heroin
— Selling drugs

After they have completed this exercise, have the students then decide what punishment they would give to the perpetrator of the crimes on the list. You may give them suggestions, such as prison, community service, capital punishment, etc. They will not be bound by the law as it stands, but they are to be the judge/jury in making the decision.

This will give you a basis from which to have the Crime Prevention Officer, should it be appropriate, explain to the class about the various categories of crimes and what usually happens to those who are arrested.

Next, have the students discuss how they are affected by crime and ask them to share any experiences they may have had as victims of crime.

Have the students devise and use a questionnaire with students, teachers and parents to find out their attitudes towards crime and how many of them have been victims. Have them publish the results and use it as a talking point about what can be done.

Perhaps the findings will indicate that theft is a problem in school. Have the students devise a plan to try to stop the problem.

This lesson may bring up strong feelings and engender disagreements about the issue of crime and how the law is/is not enforced. It is important that the students have a chance to air their views and discuss their fellings.

To follow up, the students may want to write to newspapers with their concerns or approach local radio stations about having a panel of young people present their views.

Decide if you want to have speakers come in to discuss crime, the law or other issues which arise during discussion.

8. Rights and Responsibilities

'We all have certain rights, such as the right to breathe and the right to eat. Can you name some of your rights?'

Write the students suggestions on the board. Taking this as a basis, have the students divide into groups with the task of putting these rights into three categories on which they must agree.

These categories are:

- Essential rights for everyong
- Good rights to have, but not essential
- Luxury rights

If there are not enough suggestion, use these to supplement your list:

Education
Work
Safety
The vote

Life
Fair trial
Money
Food
Home
To have children

Alternatively, have the students in small groups come up with a list of rights for each category, including the ones you have written on the board.

When the students have listed the rights in categories, have them discuss how they feel about their rights.

- Do they think that putting rights into categories works?
- What rights do they have?
- Which of those listed do they consider most essential for themselves? Their families? Their friends?
- What would they do if their rights were taken away?
- Are there countries and cultures which have a different view of people's rights? What do they think of these views?
- If we have rights, are there responsibiliites which go with the rights? For example, if we have the right to safety, what are our responsibilities if:

  a) we see a stranger, a friend or someone in our family being bullied?
  b) we see a stranger, a friend or someone in our family being racially or sexually harassed?
  c) we see a stranger, a friend or someone in our family being robbed?
  d) we see a stranger, a friend or someone in our family being attacked?

- Do we have a responsibility to do something if we see or know about:

  a) a stranger (friend, family) sniffing glue?
  b) a stranger (friend, family) smashing a shop front window?
  c) a stranger (friend, family) littering the pavement?
  d) a stranger (friend, family) creating a disturbance at a football match?

Have the students think of other situations which might raise the issue of responsibility such as:

- Under-age drinking
- Drinking/driving
- Having an elderly neighbour or relative who needs assistance
- Having a baby
- Aerosol cans and the environment
- Seeing a child fall into a river
- Having to take care of an infirm parent or relative
- Having a sibling/friend with a handicap

There are numerous examples that the students can bring up.

When the students have discussed the issues about responsibilities, have them either make up a roleplay around one of the situations of their choice showing how they might deal with the problem, or write a story or draw a picture.

This could be the basis for follow-up activities such as cutting stories from the newspaper or relating stories from the television about rights and/or responsibilities.

For the school community, perhaps a project on the rights and responsibilities of the students and staff to each other and the surrounding community would be appropriate. For example, if there is a problem with shoplifting from a local shop, what are the responsibilities of the students and/or staff? What about the shopkeeper? If there are a group of students bothering other students, what could be done?

You may want to come back to these issues as problems or queries arise throughout the year.

9. Relationships

The first part of this lesson is appropriate for all teenagers. In the second part, use the questionnaire from *Keeping Safe* for the right age group.

If you have a mixed school, separate the boys and girls. Ask that each group list:

- What qualities they look for in a friend of the same sex.
- What qualities they look for in a friend of the opposite sex.
- What qualities they look for in a date.
- What qualities they would expect from all of the above.

When the class is together, discuss the similarities and differences. The 'qualities' sometimes expected for a date include physical attractiveness or material goods. Discuss why the lists are different or the same. How are the female and male lists different or the same? Ask the boys to make comments about the girls' lists and vice versa.

Have the students break into small mixed groups to produce one list of qualities they would expect in anyone – male, female or a date. As this usually engenders much discussion, allow the groups plenty of time.

Give the students the questionnaire from *Keeping Safe* (pages 110–117). This may be photocopied out of the book for the entire class. Please note the age differences and give the appropriate questionnaire to your class. It may take 10 minutes for them to complete it.

Do not collect the questionnaire, but use it as the basis for discussion. The suggested answers are given, but as it says, these are only to be used as a guide.

Questionnaire for Young Teenagers (from *Keeping Safe, A Practical Guide to Talking with Children*, **Michelle Elliott, Hodder & Stoughton, 1988**

This questionnaire is designed to be used as a tool for communicating with young people about keeping safe from assault. It is not meant to be a test which is marked, but a way of opening up the subject without being alarmist. You may not always agree with the answers; some could be true or false depending upon the circumstances. The answers are given as a guide.

The questionnaire does not mention sex abuse or rape, but does use the word assault. It can be used with younger or less mature teens. The questionnaire on page 112 is for older teens.

Questions

1. You have the right to be safe. **T F**
2. You should always keep secrets if you promise not to tell. **T F**
3. A bribe is given to make you do something you do not want to do. **T F**
4. People are either good or bad. **T F**
5. Only bad people who look strange hurt children. **T F**
6. Adults do not always believe children. **T F**
7. Children should always obey adults. **T F**
8. You sometimes have the right to break rules. **T F**
9. It is a good idea to answer the telephone by repeating your name or your telephone number. **T F**
10. You should never lie. **T F**
11. You should never fight back if someone attacks you. **T F**
12. You have the right to tell anyone, even someone you know and trust, not to touch you in any way which makes you feel uncomfortable. **T F**
13. Jealousy is a sign of true love. **T F**
14. You should never hurt anyone's feelings. **T F**
15. Looking foolish in front of others is really embarrassing. **T F**
16. Boys are usually encouraged to be sensitive and gentle with girls. **T F**
17. When a child is assaulted, the offender is usually a stranger. **T F**
18. Girls are assaulted much more often than boys. **T F**
19. The vast majority of attackers are men. **T F**
20. The best way to escape a potential assault is to vomit. **T F**
21. A 'real man' shows the girl that he is the boss. **T F**
22. Generally the more attractive a girl is the greater her chance of being assaulted. **T F**
23. It is sometimes the victim's fault that he/she was assaulted. **T F**
24. People are much safer from assault at home. **T F**
25. If you or someone you know is assaulted, you should tell a trusted adult immediately. **T F**

Answers

1. You have the right to be safe. **True**

2. You should always keep secrets if you promise not to tell. **False**
Some secrets should not be kept. If anyone asks you to keep touching a secret or if you feel confused, uncomfortable or frightened by a secret, find a trusted adult to tell.

3. A bribe is given to make you do something you do not want to do. **True**

4. People are either good or bad. **False**

5. Only bad people who look strange hurt children. **False**

6. Adults do not always believe children. **True**
If the person you tell a problem to does not believe you, keep telling until someone does.

7. Children should always obey adults. **False**
In order to keep safe, it may be necessary to disobey an adult.

8. You sometimes have the right to break rules. **True**
To keep safe, it may be necessary to disobey an adult.

9. It is a good idea to answer the telephone by repeating your name or your telephone number. **False**

10. You should never lie. **False**
You might have to lie to keep safe. For example, you could say that your mum was waiting for you across the road if someone was bothering you.

11. You should never fight back if someone attacks you. **False**
If you feel in danger, you should do whatever you can to keep safe, such as kick, yell, bite, etc.

12. You have the right to tell anyone, even someone you know and trust, not to touch you in any way which makes you feel uncomfortable. **True**
You have the right to say who touches your body.

13. Jealousy is a sign of true love. **False**
Love depends upon mutual trust.
Jealousy is based upon lack of trust.

14. You should never hurt anyone's feelings. **False**
In order to keep yourself safe, you may have to say no to someone you know and like, which might hurt his or her feelings.

15. Looking foolish in front of others is really embarrassing. **True**
But do not be afraid to look foolish if you feel inside that something is wrong. If you think you would leave a party, for example, because you do not like what is happening, do leave even if you are embarrassed. It might keep you safe.

16 Boys are usually encouraged to be sensitive and gentle with girls. **False**
Girls should make it clear to boys that they like boys who are not afraid to be kind. Boys often think that girls only like the 'macho' type.

17. When a child is assaulted, the offender is usually a stranger. **False**
Over seventy-five per cent of people who assault children are known to the children.

18. Girls are assaulted much more often than boys. **False**
Boys are almost as much at risk as girls, though boys less often report an assault.

19. The vast majority of assaults are committed by men. **True**
Over ninety per cent of reported assaults are committed by men. However, most men would never attack anyone.

20. The best way to escape a potential assault is to vomit. **False**
While it may work, conversations with offenders indicate that these kinds of tactics make them angry, rather than disgusted. Many people feel that an immediate spirited physical self-defence, including loud yelling, kicking, hitting, etc., is best because the element of surprise helps the victim to get away. Some people have successfully talked their way out of dangerous situations. Each person must decide what is best according to the circumstances.

21. A 'real man' shows the girl that he is the boss. **False**
Why should one partner be boss?

22. Generally the more attractive a girl is the greater her chance of being assaulted. **False**
Studies have shown that being physically attractive has nothing to do with assault.

23. It is sometimes the victim's fault that he/she was assaulted. **False**
It is always the offender's fault. No one deserves to be assaulted.

24. People are much safer from assault at home. **False**
In a recent London survey, fifty-one per cent of assaults happened either in the victim's or the assailant's home.

25. If you or someone you know is assaulted, you should tell a trusted adult immediately. **True**
Think about people who would believe you and who would help you make a decision about what to do. An assault is too big a burden to carry in secret and getting help early will often lessen the trauma.

Questionnaire for Older Teenagers

One way to begin talking with young people about keeping safe from sexual abuse and assault is to give them this questionnaire or take it with them. It is not meant to be a quiz to be marked, but a basis for communication. Although answers are given, in some cases you may disagree with the answer. The desired outcome should be that teenagers think about and plan what to do should they be placed in a dangerous situation. This isn't a contest to get the 'right' answer.

This questionnaire does mention the terms sex abuse and rape and should be used with more mature teenagers.

Questions

1. You have the right to tell anyone, even someone you know and trust, not to touch you in any way which makes you feel uncomfortable. **T F**

2. When a girl says 'no' to a boy, she frequently means 'yes'. **T F**

3. A boy has a right to expect more than a kiss after he has spent money on a date. **T F**

4. Jealousy is a sign of true love. **T F**

5. Birth control is the female's responsibility **T F**

6. Boys are not encouraged to be sensitive and gentle with girls. **T F**

7. Sexual frustration can be physically harmful. **T F**

8. People who fantasise about being seduced or raped have emotional problems. **T F**

9. Most date rapes occur because a girl teases a boy to the point that he cannot control himself. **T F**

10. Alcohol and/or drugs can lower inhibitions about engaging in sexual activity. **T F**

11. When a child is molested, the molester is usually a stranger. **T F**

12. Girls are molested much more often than boys. **T F**

13. The vast majority of sexual abusers are men. **T F**

14. The best way to escape a potential rapist is to vomit. **T F**

15. A 'real man' shows the girl that he is the boss. **T F**

16. Generally the more attractive a girl is the higher her chance of being sexually assaulted. **T F**

17. When a girl is sexually assaulted, she usually has done something to provoke it. **T F**

18. It is against the law for a boy to engage in sexual intercourse with a girl under sixteen, even with her consent. **T F**

19. Sexual gratification is the major reason for rape. **T F**

20. Males who are sexually assaulted suffer the same kind of emotional trauma as female victims. **T F**

21. People are much safer from sexual assault at home. **T F**

22. Less than half of all rapes are reported to the police. **T F**
23. An assailant rarely finds it necessary to use a weapon to commit rape. **T F**
24. People who sexually assault others are psychologically disturbed. **T F**
25. Rapists are secret, solitary offenders who usually attack their victims when the rapist is alone. **T F**
26. Teenage and adult victims of sexual assault seldom know the identity of the offender. **T F**
27. Sexual assault is usually an unplanned, spontaneous act. **T F**
28. There are many false reports of rape by women seeking revenge on their boyfriends. **T F**
29. If female victim feels uncomfortable talking with a male police officer, she has the right to request that a female officer is called. **T F**
30. Since the rape victim is often unprotected by contraceptives, she will probably become pregnant. **T F**
31. The victim is allowed to have a friend stay with her during the medical examination or questioning. **T F**
32. During an investigation of a rape, the victim can refuse to answer questions irrelevant to the rape. **T F**
33. If a woman is raped, her name will be published by the media reporting her case. **T F**
34. As a rule, the rape victim can be asked questions in court about her sexual conduct. **T F**
35. If you or someone you know has been sexually assaulted, you should tell a trusted adult immediately. **T F**

Answers

1. You have the right to tell anyone, even someone you know and trust, not to touch you in any way which makes you feel uncomfortable. **True**
   Since a high percentage of the assaults on teenagers are by an adult known to them, it is important to learn to say no not only to strangers, but to friends, family members or acquaintances.

2. When a girl says 'no' to a boy, she frequently means 'yes'. **False**
   This attitude is left over from old films and books. Boys and girls should discuss together their ideas about mixed messages so that both understand the expectations and the misconceptions of the other.

3. A boy has a right to expect more than a kiss after he has spent money on a date. **False**
   If this is his attitude, 'go Dutch'.

4. Jealousy is a sign of true love. **False**
   Love depends upon mutual trust. Jealousy is based upon lack of trust.

5. Birth control is the female's responsibility. **False**
   It should be a shared responsibility.

6. Boys are not encouraged to be sensitive and gentle with girls. **True**
   Most boys are raised to believe that being tough and macho is what girls expect of them. This should be discussed so that girls and boys can decide what they value in a relationship.

7. Sexual frustration can be physically harmful. **False**
   Boys have used this line for years!

8. People who fantasise about being seduced or raped have emotional problems. **False**
   Some people have 'seduction' fantasies. In the fantasy, they are in control; they choose the 'assailant', place, circumstances, etc. The reality of rape is different – violent and sadistic.

9. Most date rapes occur because a girl teases the boy to the point that he cannot control himself. **False**
   This attitude blames the victim. Rape occurs because the assailant has problems with anger, aggression, hostility and power.

10. Alcohol and/or drugs can lower inhibitions about engaging in sexual activity. **True**
    Studies have shown this to be true for both sexes.

11. When a child is molested, the molester is usually a stranger. **False**
    The child knows the attacker in at least seventy-five per cent of the reported cases of child molestation.

12. Girls are molested much more often than boys. **False**
    Statistics vary, but boys are almost as much at risk as girls. The victimisation of boys is reported less often, partly because of the fear of being branded as a homosexual after an attack.

13. The vast majority of sexual abusers are men. **True**
    Ninety per cent of reported attacks were committed by men.

14. The best way to escape a potential rapist is to vomit. **False**
    While it may work, conversations with convicted rapists indicate that these kinds of tactics make them angry, rather than disgusted. Many people feel that an immediate spirited physical defence, including loud yelling, kicking, hitting, etc. is best because the element of surprise would help the victim to get away. Some people have successfully talked their way out of rape, but each must decide for herself according to the circumstances.

15. A 'real man' shows the girl that he is the boss. **False**
    Why should one partner be the boss? This implies that the girl is incapable of directing her own life. It places her in the same category as a docile pet.

16. Generally the more attractive a girl is the higher her chance of being sexually assaulted. **False**
    Studies of assault victims have shown that being

physically attractive has nothing to do with sexual assault.

17. When a girl is sexually assaulted, she usually has done something to provoke it.   **False**
In the United States, the National Commission on the Causes and Prevention of Violence did a study on crimes of violence and paid particular attention to the role of the victim in cases of murder, assault, robbery and rape. The commission wanted to determine whether victims of these crimes in any way provoked them or rashly touched off the action against them. It was discovered that victims of rape were responsible for less provocative behaviour or unwitting collusion than victims of murder, assault or robber. The cases on file of the rape of individuals of all ages, from three-month-old babies to ninety-seven-year-old women, show how ridiculous this myth really is.

18. It is against the law for a boy to engage in sexual intercourse with a girl under sixteen, even with her consent.   **True**
The legal age of consent is sixteen.

19. Sexual gratification is the major reason for rape.   **False**
Rape is about violence, not sex. If you hit someone over the head with your rolling pin, it is not called cooking.

20. Males who are sexually assaulted suffer the same kind of emotional trauma as female victims.   **True**
Sexual assaults on males is reported even less than assault on females and there is no support system, such as Rape Crisis Centres, for male victims.

21. People are much safer from sexual assault at home.   **False**
In a recent London survey, fifty-one per cent of sexual assaults happened either in the victim's or the assailant's home.

22. Less than half of all rapes are reported to the police.   **True**
Only one in twelve are reported, according to the London survey.

23. An assailant rarely finds it necessary to use a weapon to commit rape.   **True**
Only a small proportion of sexual assaults involve weapons. Most assailants use superior size and fear to subdue victims.

24. People who sexually assault others are psychologically disturbed.   **False**
Most test as 'normal' on psychological tests.

25. Rapists are secret, solitary offenders who usually attack their victims when the rapist is alone.   **True**
In only one in a hundred cases in the London survey was there more than one assailant.

26. Teenage and adult victims seldom know the identity of the rapist.   **False**
Over sixty per cent of attacks in the London survey were known to the victim.

27. Sexual assault is usually an unplanned, spontaneous act. **False**
   Most sexual assaults are planned.

28. There are many false reports of rape by women seeking revenge on their boyfriends. **False**
   In a study in New York of all the reported rapes in one year, only two per cent turned out to be false.

29. If a female victim feels uncomfortable talking with a male police officer, she has the right to request that a female officer be called. **True**
   While a victim has the right to request this, the police have no obligation to provide a female officer. The police do try to comply with this request, if at all possible.

30. Since the rape victim is often unprotected by contraceptives, she will probably become pregnant. **False**
   Only a small percentage of rape victims become pregnant.

31. The victim is allowed to have a friend stay with her during the medical examination or questioning. **True**
   This can be a family member or close friend.

32. During an investigation of a rape, the victim can refuse to answer questions irrelevant to the rape. **True**
   Questions about a victim's personal life, not relevant to the rape, need not be answered.

33. If a woman is raped, her name will be published by the media reporting her case. **False**
   Rape victims are entitled to anonymity before, during and after the trial.

34. As a rule, the rape victim can be asked questions in court about her sexual conduct. **False**
   In court a rape victim may not be asked questions about her previous sexual conduct unless the judge is satisfied that these questions are relevant to the defence.

35. If you or someone you know has been sexually assaulted, you should tell a trusted adult immediately. **True**
   Think about the people who would believe you and who would help you in making a decision about what to do. Sexual assault is too big a burden to carry in secret and getting supportive help early will often lessen the trauma. If you feel completely alone, telephone the local Rape Crisis Centre (the number is in the directory) or telephone the London office on (01) 837 1600 for information. Childline, on 0800 1111, is a 24 hour telephone service for children or teenagers in distress.

10. Abuse

Ask the students to divide into groups and spend ten minutes defining what they consider to be abuse. Many of them will have heard the terms physical and sexual abuse from the television, radio or from discussions with family and friends. Having the students define abuse avoids the problem of giving them too much information (in case of younger students particularly).

Take their definitions and compile a list of their ideas. You will probably find that they include:

- Beating
- Burning
- Biting
- Hitting
- Rape
- Sexual abuse
- Starvation

With younger students, do not use the terms of rape and sexual abuse unless they do. You will probably find that they know the terms, but parents may object if you *introduce* concepts that their teenagers are not ready to understand.

Ask the students to define the various forms of abuse (listed below). Ask groups to find definitions from books, newspaper articles, television programmes, etc.

If the students ask you for your definition of abuse, you can use your own or the following:

Physical Abuse:

'Physical abuse implies physically harmful action directed against a child; it is usually defined by an inflicted injury such as bruises, burns, head injuries, fractures, abdominal injuries, or poisoning.' C.H. Kempe

Sexual Abuse:

'Sexual abuse is any exploitation of children under the age of 16 for the sexual pleasure, gratification or profit of an adult or significantly older person.

This ranges from obscene telephone calls, indecent exposure (flashing), taking pornographic pictures, attempted intercourse, rape or incest.' (From *Keeping Safe* by Michele Elliott)

Emotional Abuse:

'Emotional abuse includes a child being continually terrorised, berated or rejected.' C.H. Kempe

Neglect:

'Neglect can be a very insidious form of maltreatment, which can go on for a long time. It implies the failure of the parents to act properly in safe-guarding the health, safety and well-being of the child. It includes nutritional neglect, failure to provide medical care or to protect a child from physical and social danger.' C.H. Kempe

All those forms of abuse can be related. For example, a child who is physically abused is also emotionally abused. The students can discuss how abuse is interrelated.

Ask the students what their concerns are about the various forms of abuse. Does it make them sad, angry, confused when they hear about a young child being abused in some way?

• What do they think should be done to protect children?
• What are their views about the people who abuse children?
• What would they suggest to *help* an abuser who was their own age?

You could ask the students to write a report about a recent newspaper case of abuse, chosen by them. They could also do group work and come up with an oral report for the class about how their group feels and what they think should happen.

The students could set up a trial regarding a case of abuse and decide how they would change the laws or if they would leave them as they were with regard to abuse of children.

These exercises give the students a chance to express their feelings and concerns before going on to talk about protecting themselves from abuse. Try not to focus too heavily on just sexual abuse as it is important to discuss all forms of abuse.

Listed below are some cases of abuse which could be used as the basis of class discussion. It is better to have students bring in cases but these are listed as additional material.

Cases:

These cases have all been reported in the media. The names and some of the details have been slightly altered to protect students in the unlikely event that the people concerned are familiar to someone in the local community.

CHILD MURDERED BY FOSTER FATHER
A foster father accused of murdering a two-year-old boy was remanded in custody today. The man, G. Simmons, aged 31, is also accused of causing the boy's sister grievous bodily harm.

According to social services, both children had behavioural problems and had a tendency to inflict injuries on themselves. Their natural parents had abused the children.

Doctors said the boy had suffered severe non-accidental wounding, including haemorrhaging, indicating severe shaking, grip marks around his elbow and knee, and bruising of the jaw, consistent with being hit. There were also burn marks on the body from cigarettes.

The case has been adjourned until October.

PRISON FOR SCOUT MASTER
A scout master was jailed for three months yesterday after admitting repeatedly indecently assaulting teenage boys after getting them drunk.

M. Taylor, aged 46, a pillar of society and a respected member of his community, abused six boys between the ages of 13 and 16.

His crime was discovered after one of the boys told senior officials what had happened.

When passing sentence, the judge said that parents and children needed to be protected from this sort of abuse and that Mr Taylor was a danger to young boys.

CHILD LOCKED IN CUPBOARD

Police discovered a six-year-old girl chained by the ankle and locked in a three- by two-foot cupboard under the stairs. The child is suffering from malnutrition and appears unable to talk or walk properly. The girl has burns and sores over most of her body and has been admitted to hospital.

The girl's parents said the child was 'always a problem and never did what she was told'. They have been arrested.

A police officer said today that it was the worst case of child abuse he had seen in 20 years.

Follow-up activities

Use Appendix 4.2 to discuss how media images might affect the problem of child sexual abuse.

11. Keeping Safe from Abuse

Note to teacher: When presenting this to younger teens, do not use the term sexual abuse unless the parents have agreed.

You may find that the students are not bothered and will use the terms freely, but that parents are concerned. Follow whatever guidelines you have worked out with the parents and the Board of Governors. You can use the term abuse or assault.

'Talking about staying safe from abuse sometimes makes people nervous. You might feel like laughing or telling jokes or just acting silly. Remember that we need to be sensitive to one another when discussing these issues. Some research has shown that as many as 1 in 10 young people has a (sexually) abusive experience before reaching the age of 16. There may be people in this class who have been abused and it is not funny to be abused, either physically or sexually or emotionally. First let's find out what you know about the problem.'

Write on the board:

WHO   WHERE   WHEN   WHY

Ask the students to divide into small groups and come up with a list of who the abusers are, who the victims are, where abuse happens, when it happens and finally why they think it happens. This can take a whole lesson or you can put a time limit on it. It usually takes at least 20 to 30 minutes.

The students may tackle one form of abuse and you can repeat the exercise for other forms, or you may have them combine the various forms of abuse. It tends to work better if they do one at a time, but how you teach it will depend upon the time you have and their interests.

When the students have compiled their lists, write their ideas on the board under the headings. Taking sexual abuse as an example, it may look something like:

WHO	WHERE/WHEN	WHY
OFFENDER		
Druggies	Dark	For kicks
Weirdos	Alleys	Hatred
Maniacs	Lifts	Power
Men	Parks	Can't help it
Strangers	Cars	Sex
Women	Deserted places	Crazy
Teachers	Home	
Doctors	Friend's house	
Parents		
Someone known		
Acquantainces		
VICTIMS		
Girls		
Women		
Prostitutes		
Children		
Boys		
Old ladies		

When everything is written on the board, go back and circle the MOST common factors:

- Most (75%) of the offenders are known to the victims.
- The reported offenders are mainly male (95%). Here emphasise that that does not mean that most men abuse people and that there are hardly any reported cases of female abusers.
- Although there are more reported girls as victims, many experts in the field feel that boys just do not report abuse.
- Most abuse or assaults take place in the home of the victim or in the home of the offender.
- Most offenders appear to be quite normal and come from every class, race, occupation and background.

For physical abuse, the profile would probably emphasise parents, though being beaten up by a stranger would also be physical abuse.

Be certain to state that it is not always possible to say 'No' and get away and that sometimes people have no choice. This is in case a student in your class has already been abused so s/he will not feel responsible for what happened.

'It is never your fault if you are abused, but there are some possible strategies which could work to either avoid a difficult or dangerous situation or which might help if you find yourself in such a situation. Some of these we have discussed in previous lessons, others may be new ideas from you.'

Have the students brainstorm what they might do if someone tried to abuse/assault them or what they would do if it did happen (i.e. getting help).

Students may come up with ideas such as:

- Tell a friend. (Suggest that the friend helps them to tell someone else like a school nurse or a parent or another trusted adult.)
- Kick the attacker. (Perhaps, but make sure you can get away.)
- Yell.
- Get away.

Allow all suggestions, as some may help a student who needs to tell to decide what to do. We can only suggest to students what they may do. The ultimate choice to *tell* about abuse is with them. Otherwise, adults can only act upon symptoms and suspicions.

12. Getting Help

Where would you turn if you were worried about a case of abuse or drug-taking or an alcohol problem or anorexia or gambling or AIDS? Have the students try to come up with all the sources they can contact.

In the back of this manual there is a list which could be used if necessary to supplement the list the students compile. However, it is best that the students do their own research as far as possible.

Ask the students to brainstorm how they could use the information they have gathered. Suggestions might include making posters to put up around the school or community, or producing a leaflet for the students to use.

Knowing where to turn if there is a problem is a useful basis for all the lessons. This lesson can be used on its own or as a follow-up to any chapter by just asking the students to research help for that particular topic.

Where to Get Help

The decision about getting outside help must be made according to the circumstances. Parents or other interested adults can contact either the local social services, a GP or the police. (Please note that if local authorities receive information suggesting that there are grounds for bringing care proceedings in respect of a child or young person, they have a statutory duty to investigate the case unless they consider it unnecessary.) Your church or local religious organisation may also be helpful. In addition, there are several organisations listed below that offer help and advice. If you want to know the policy of the help organisation about reporting, ask before you proceed.

Abuse

United Kingdom

Childline. Freepost 1111 (no stamp needed), London EC4 4BB. 0800 1111
24 hour charge-free telephone counselling and advice service for children in trouble or danger.

Child Helpline. (0742) 886886.
Offers telephone advice and support for children around the Sheffield area who are victims of abuse.

Family Contact Line. (061) 941 4066, 10am to 10pm.
Provides a telephone listening service to families, and nursery facilities.

Family Network. c/o National Children's Home, 85 Highbury Park, London N5 1UD.
Scotland: (041) 221 6722; Wales: (0222) 29461; north of England: (061) 236 9873; south of England: (0582) 422751.
Provides help for children and families with problems. There is a telephone counselling service.

In Support of Sexually Abused Children. Angela Rivera, PO Box 526, London NW6 1SU, (081) 202 3024.
Offers support for sexually abused children and their parents.

Linkline. (081) 645 0505.
Linkline is under the umbrella of OPUS. It is a 24 hour ansaphone for distress calls which gives numbers of groups on call when the office is unattended.

Mothers of Abused Children. Chris Strickland, (0965) 31432, Cumbria.
Support offered for mothers of sexually abused children.

National Society for the Prevention of Cruelty to Children. Head Office, 64–74 Saffron Hill, London EC1N 8RS, (071) 242 1626.
The Society operates in England, Northern Ireland and Wales. See directory for local branches.
The NSPCC aims to prevent child abuse in all forms and to give practical help to families with children at risk.

Organisation for Parents Under Stress (OPUS). 106 Godstone Road, Whyteleafe, Surrey CR3 0EB, (081) 645 0469.
OPUS has a network of thirty self-help groups for parents under stress to prevent child abuse and maltreatment of infants and young children.

Parents Against Injustice (PAIN). 'Conifers', 2 Pledgdon Green, Nr. Henham, Bishop's Stortford, Herts. (0279) 850545.
Gives advice to parents who feel they have been wrongly accused of abusing their children.

Parents Anonymous. 6 Manor Gardens, London N7 6LA, (071) 263 8918, 6pm to 6am.
Parents Anonymous offers help to parents who are tempted to

abuse their children and to those who have already done so.
There are meetings and a telephone counselling and visiting
service for parents by trained volunteer parents.

Rape Crisis Centres. For information on local branches,
telephone (071) 837 1600 or write to PO Box 69, London WC1
9NJ.

**Royal Scottish Society for the Prevention of Cruelty to
Children.** Melville House, 41 Polwarth Terrace, Edinburgh
EH11 1NU, (031) 337 8539/8530.

Samaritans. See directory for local numbers.
Samaritans are trained volunteers who talk with people about
problems of depression and suicide.

Touchline. (0532) 457777.
9.30am to 9.30pm, Mon–Fri. Telephone listening service for
anyone who has been abused. Located in the Leeds area.

Woman's Therapy Centre. 6 Manor Gardens, London N7 6LA,
(071) 263 6200.
Send a large SAE for list of groups and activities.

Irish Republic

Irish Society for the Prevention of Cruelty to Children. 20
Molesworth Street, Dublin 2, Irish Republic (0001) 760423/4/5.

Australia

Adelaide: Crisis Care, (08) 272 1222   24 hours

Brisbane: Crisis Care, (07) 224 6855   24 hours

Canberra: Children's Services, (062) 462625   9am to 5pm

Darwin: Department for Community Development, (089) 814 733

Hobart: Department for Community Welfare,
Crisis Intervention, (002) 302529   24 hours

Melbourne: Protective Services for Children,
(03) 309 5700   9am to 5pm

Perth: Crisis Care, (09) 321 4144 or
(008) 199 008 (toll free)   24 hours

Sydney: Child Protection and Family Crisis.
(02) 818 5555   24 hours
2UE Kids Careline, (02) 929 7799   9am to 5pm, Mon–Fri

You can also contact through your local directory:
the Police
Lifeline
Rape Crisis Centres

New Zealand

Auckland: Help, Auckland 399 185   24 hours

AIDS

Your GP or paedetrician should be able to give you advice and can arrange for testing, if necessary.

For free leaflets and booklets, contact your local health education unit, which is listed in the directory under the name of your Health Authority.

To obtain a copy of the British Medical Associations's seventy page illustrated guide entitled AIDS and You, Send £1.95 to: British Medical Association. Tavistock Square, London WC1H 9JP.

You can also contact:

Health Call. 0898 600 699, gives recorded general information on AIDS. 0898 600 900, gives recorded specific information on AIDS.

The Haemophilia Society. 123 Westminster Bridge Road, London SE1 7HR, (071) 405 1010.

The Society will offer advice to people with haemophilia or to the parents of haemophiliac children.

Healthline Telephone Service. (081) 981 2717, (081) 980 7222 or from outside London, dial (0345) 581151 and your call will be charged at local rates.

The Healthline gives recorded information and advice about AIDS, safer sex, drug abuse and blood transfusions. 24 hour service.

Terrence Higgins Trust. BM/AIDS, London WC1N 3XX. (071) 833 2971. Monday to Friday 7pm to 10pm, Saturday/Sunday 3pm to 10pm.

Offers help and counselling to people with HIV virus or AIDS.

Alcohol

For help with dealing with alcohol abuse, contact:

Al-Anon/Al-Teen. 61 Great Dover Street, London SE1 4YF, (071) 403 0888.

For family, friends and children who have a relative affected by drinking problems.

Alcoholics Anonymous. PO Box 1, Stonebow house, Stonebow, York YO1 2NJ.

Alcohol Counselling Service (ACS). 34 Electric Lane, London SW9 8JJ, (071) 737 3579/3570.

Anorexia/Bulminia

Anorexia and Bulminia Nervosa Association. Tottenham Women's Health Centre, Annexe C, Tottenham Town Hall, London N5 4RX.

Anorexia Aid. The Priory Centre, 11 Priory Road, High Wycombe, Bucks HP13 6SL.

Anorexia Family Aid and National Information Centre. Sackville Place, 44/48 Magdalen Street, Norwich, Norfolk NR3 1JE.

Bereavement

Bereaved Parents Helpline. 6 Canons Gate, Harlow, Essex, (0279) 412745.
Offers support to parents by telephone and by making visits locally.

Compassionate Friends. 6 Denmark Street, Bristol, BS1 5DQ. (0272) 292778.
Offers friendship to parents whose children have died through accident, illness, murder or suicide. Local groups throughout the country.

Contraception

For advice on contraception, pregnancy, or abortion, contact:

The British Pregnancy Advisory Service. 7 Belgrave Road, London SW1V 1QB, (071) 222 0985.

Brook Advisory Centres (for young people). Head Office, 153a East Street, London SE17 2SD, (071) 708 1234.

Family Planning Association. 27 Mortimer Street, London W1N 7RJ, (071) 636 7866.

Counselling

These organisations offer counselling on family and other problems:

Family Network Services. c/o National Children's Home, Stephenson Hall, 85c Highbury Park, London N5 1UD.

Birmingham: (021) 440 5970	Luton: (052) 422751
Cardiff: (0222) 29461	Maidstone: (0622) 56677
Glasgow: (041) 221 6722	Manchester: (061) 236 9873
Glenrothes: (0592) 759651	Norwich: (0603) 660679
Gloucester: (0452) 24019	Preston: (0772) 24006
Leeds: (0532) 456456	Swansea: (0792) 292798
London: (081) 514 1177	Taunton: (0823) 73191

National Association of Young People's Counselling and Advisory Service (for young people). 17–23 Albion Street, Leicester LE1 6GD, (0533) 554775.

Drugs

Doctors, Social Services, Police and Citizens Advice Bureaux should be able to advise about local services.

For information about drug advice centres, dial 100 and ask for Freephone 'Drug Problems'.

Leaflets about drugs are available from:

Dept DM, DHSS Leaflets Unit, PO Box 21, Stanmore, Middlesex HA7 1AY.

- What every parent should know about drugs (DM 1)
- Drugs: what parents can do (DM2)
- Drug misuse: A basic briefing (DM 3)
- Drugs, What You Can Do as a Parent (DM4)

The Department of Education and Science and Welsh Office also produce leaflets and booklets about drugs available in English and Welsh from:

Welsh Office. Information Division, Cathays Park, Cardiff CF1 3NQ.

To obtain a leaflet on Solvent Abuse:

Solvent Abuse. Dept. M50, 13–39 Standard Road, London NW10

- What to do about glue-sniffing

Standing Conference on Drug Abuse (SCODA). Kingsbury House, 1–4 Hatton Place, Hatton Garden, London EC1N 8ND, (071) 430 2341.
Will supply a list of local services available throughout the country.

Families Anonymous. 88 Caledonian Road, London N7 9DN, (071) 731 8060.
Provide information about self-help groups for concerned parents.

Drugs Education

Teachers Advisory Counsel on Alcohol and Drug Education (TACADE). 2 Mount Street, Manchester M2 SN9.
Provides education and training materials for the formal education system. Write for a full list of materials.

The Society for the Prevention of Solvent Abuse (RE-SOLV). St. Mary's Chambers, 19 Station Road, Stone, Staffordshire ST15 8JP, (0795) 817885, (0785) 46097.
RE-SOLV produces teaching programmes to help encourage young people to resist experimentation. Has videos and books available. For a full list of resources, send a large SAE.

Gambling

Parents of Young Gamblers. Memorial School, Mount Street, Taunton, Somerset TA1 3QB, (0823) 256936.

Gamblers Anonymous. 17–23 Blantyre Street, London SW10 0DT, (071) 352 3060.
Contact either of the above organisations for help and advice about gambling problems.

Legal Advice

The Children's Legal Centre. 20 Compton Terrace, London N1 2UN, (071) 359 6251.
Gives advice about law and policy affecting children and young people in England and Wales.

Citizen's Advice Bureau.
Will give you details of services available and advice about how to get help. Listed in your local directory.

Runaways

In addition to the police, contact the Salvation Army for help and advice if your child has run away.

The Central London Teenage Project. c/o The Church of England Children's Society, Edward Rudolf House, Margery Street, London WC1X 0JL, (071) 837 4299.
They have a 'Safe House' for runaways and will pass on messages. They will not, however, give the runaway's location.

Self-Defence

Contact your library or your local council for information about self-defence classes in your area.

The Metropolitan Special Constabulary. New Scotland Yard, London SW1H 0BG.

The Self-Defence Project. Women's Education Resource Centre, Princeton Street, London WC1R 4BH, (071) 242 6807.

The Suzy Lamplugh Trust. 14 East Sheen Avenue, London SW14 8AS, (081) 876 1839.
The trust has produced a video for those who work with the public and may find themselves in a dangerous situation. The video explains how to recognise and try to talk your way out of danger or what to do if you have to defend yourself. £30 from Citizens Advice Bureaux or contact the Trust.

Telephones

'Nuisance Callers': a leaflet giving guidance on dealing with abusive or nuisance telephone calls. Available free from British Telecom Customer Service.

Tranquilisers

Come Off It. 61 Holly Avenue, Jesmond, Newcastle-upon-Tyne NE6 5EA, (091) 281 1004.

Life Without Tranquilisers. Lynmouth, Devon EX35 6EE. Send SAE for information and advice about problems caused by tranquilisers or sleeping tablets.

Tranquiliser Recovery and New Existence (TRANX). 17 Peel Road, Harrow, Middlesex, HA1 2EZ, (01) 427 2065 and (01) 427 2827.

Victim Support

Victim Support. Head Office, Cranmer House, 39 Brixton Road, London SW9 6DZ, (01) 735 9166.
A nationwide network of support groups offering practical help to victims of violence and crime. You can find out about your local branch by contacting the above office.

13. Common Sense Self-Defence

Make sure that you have parental agreement if you are going to teach teenagers any form of physical self-defence.

Please note that in the lessons that follow the attackers are referred to as male and female. This is to ensure that the students are aware that an attacker can be either male or female.

'The best form of self-defence is to get away from a dangerous situation as quickly as possible and to avoid getting into dangerous situations. Can you think of some common sense ideas for avoiding danger?'
Suggestions:

- Avoid taking short-cuts through dark or deserted places.
- Never hitch-hike.
- If someone approaches you asking directions, keep your distance or walk away and pretend not to hear.
- If you are threatened, yell and run away, if possible.
- If you are being followed, go into a shop or towards people. Try crossing the road to see if the person follows.
- Do not wear a personal stereo as it prevents you being aware of what is happening around you.
- Avoid empty carriages on trains.
- On buses or the underground, sit near the driver or guard.

The students should come up with their own suggestions, but use these if necessary:

- If you are attacked, think of what you might do. Would you talk your way out of it or pretend to do what you are asked, while waiting for a chance to get away? Only you can decide what to do in the event.

- If you do have to defend yourself, take a deep breath and try not to panic. Use anything you have to hand to defend yourself – keys, an umbrella, the heel of your shoe, hairspray.
- Remember that anything you do or any weapon you use is to provide you with an opportunity to get away. Unless you are trained in self-defence, it is absolutely senseless to stay around.
- If you are faced with a knife or another weapon, probably your best defence is to remain calm and try to talk your way out. Whatever you do, it must be your decision.
- If someone grabs your arms with her hands, jerk your arm away in the direction of her thumbs – this is the weakers part of anyone's grip.
- If someone grabs you from behind, bend forward and come back quickly, slamming your head against his face or chin (the back of your head is very hard, but it may hurt you as well).
- If there is a weapon and you think you have a chance to do something to get away, scrape your heel down the inside of her lower leg, or kick her in the knee HARD. Then stamp on her instep with all your weight. Then run!
- Kicking someone in the genitals or poking them in the eyes is not as easy as you might have heard. If you kick up at an attacker, he may just grab your leg and you will end up on the ground. If you try to poke someone in the eye, remember that the juices from the eye will get under your fingernail and be very squishy! If I hear you saying 'yuck' then do not try it. Only ever try something you can carry through with or you might just do enough to make the attacker even more angry.
- The best advice is to practise the two or three techniques you think you could use until they are automatic.
- Finally, if you are attacked, tell someone – ring the police, talk to a parent, a teacher, a friend. Do not keep it to yourself.

14. Addiction

The purpose of this lesson or lessons is to provide an introduction from which to study particular areas, such as drug abuse problems, in more depth and in the context of addition.

a) 'What is addiction?'

Write the definitions from the students on the board and discuss. If you need a definition to work with:
Addiction is a compulsive behaviour or activity which the addict cannot control or give up. The addiction meets some perceived need of the addict.

b) 'What are some forms of addiction?'

Have the students break into small groups for five minutes and brainstorm. Compile their ideas on the board.

If you need to supplement their suggestions:

Alcohol	Gambling
Cigarettes	Sex
Cannabis	Cleanliness (Obsessive)
Crack	Eating
Cocaine	Shopping
Solvents	Lying
Herion	Stealing/Shoplifting
Marijuana	Bullying
Aspirin	Work

c) 'Why do some people become addicts?'

Again, have the students do group work, but allow enough time for them to come up with at least five reasons.
The addict may be feeling some of the following:

Insecure	Guilty
Vulnerable	Humiliated
Lonely	Picked on
Unhappy	Distrustful
Unloved	Powerless
Rejected	Self-hatred
Ashamed	Depressed
Confused	Curious

'Although people who become addicts are usually desperately looking for a way to feel good, it is possible that the addiction started because they were curious about 'trying' something such as drugs which were offered to them. To continue with the addictive habit, however, indicates a basic problem such as those we have listed.'

Have the students brainstorm what people think they get out of the addictive habit, whatever that habit may be.
Suggestions:

Comfort
Identity
Self-confidence
Support
Power
Love

d) 'What do YOU think addicts get from their addiction?'
Suggestions:

More problems
Become dependent
Lose more control
Depressed

e) 'What do people need in order not to become addicts?'
Suggestions:

Love
Security
To know that it is alright to be vulnerable
Guidelines
Friends
To feel happy or satisfied
To feel a sense of accomplishment

If students can begin to understand the reasons for addictive behaviour, it will help them to put the problem of drugs into context. To follow up on this idea, have the students prioritise how they feel about the various forms of addiction, which they listed earlier (page 131). Put the words such as work, cannabis, cleanliness, cigarettes on separate pieces of paper. Working in groups, agree as a group on which addictions are the 'worst' and which are the 'best'. This should provoke discussion about how people deal with addictive behaviours and how those behaviours affect the people around them.

When the students have prioritised, have each group report back to the class. Discuss the differences in the priorities listed by the groups.

'If someone you lived with was addicted, which of these addictions would affect you the most? The least? Why?'

'How can people who are addicted be helped'.

Without the underlying problems being sorted out, people who are addicted will substitute one addiction for another. For example, giving up cigarettes may lead to over-eating of boiled sweets; giving up the liquid drug of alcohol may lead to taking on another comforter such as incessant exercise. One question here, is what are 'acceptable' addictive behaviours – something the students will have discussed when prioritising.

In order to help the students answer the question about helping addicts, you may want to encourage the students to investigate the various forms of addiction and have local experts come in to talk.

Have the students choose which areas of addiction they would like to find out more about and ask them to report to the class. Sources of further information are included in the Resources section at the end of this manual.

15. Gambling

'What is gambling?'

'Why do you think that it can be a problem for young people'.

'Without mentioning names, could anyone here talk about someone they know who might have had a gambling problem, like being addicted to arcade machines?'

If the students are having difficulty with the concept of gambling, perhaps the following story will help stimulate discussion:

David started playing fruit machines just for fun at the age of 11. At first he played in his spare time, after school and at the weekends. By the time he was 12, he began to miss the odd day of school to go to the arcades. Now he is 15 and he spends most of his time compulsively playing machines. He has lost 2 stone in weight, his eyes are bloodshot and he has stolen over £10,000 to pay for his habit. He is also aggressive and withdrawn.

'This is a true story, but the name of the boy has been changed. If you were David's parent, what signs would you think might have warned you that David had a gambling problem?'

Have the students talk in small groups and ask them to come up with a list of three or four possible signs or symptoms which might alert them to the problem. When they have finished, bring them together and write their suggestions on the board. They might include:

- Money disappearing
- Possessions disappearing or being sold
- Borrowing money
- Bloodshot eyes
- Lying
- Missing school
- Withdrawn
- Aggressive

Ask the students what they would do if their child was exhibiting these signs.

'What would you do if you knew that your little brother was gambling and stealing money to do it?'

'What would you do if your best friend was addicted to using fruit machines?'

'What are the laws regarding fruit machines and video arcades?'

Have a group of students investigate the current legislation.

Some possible sources of information are listed in the Resources section of this manual.

Have the students take all the information they acquire and:

- Suggest changes in the laws which might protect young people
- Design posters which give other students information which might be helpful
- Invite a speaker from one of the organisations which deal with gambling (see 'Getting Help' lesson)
- Do a school survey about gambling and publish the results

Students may also be affected by the gambling of a parent and it is important to make sure that they are aware of the help organisations.

Appendix 4.1   <u>MY DIARY</u>

<u>A fact/fiction story by Nicholas Hargreaves</u>

<u>Tuesday 7th September 1984</u>

My first day back at school. I got pinned down in the
playground and tortured. That's what it's like everyday. Big boys
in the seventh year look like giants to me. They prod and tickle
me. I went to see the headmaster, Mr Clay, who just laughed and
sent me to my lesson.

<u>Wednesday 8th September</u>

Prod! Poke! Thump! "Ouch!"

<u>Thursday 9th September</u>

Prod! Poke! Thump! "Ouch!"

<u>Friday 10th September</u>

Prod! Poke! Thump! "Ouch!"

<u>Wednesday 15th September</u>

Everyday's the same. I get bullied day in; day out. I can't help it,
it's not my fault.
Going on a nature trip today. Get away from those bullies.
Mark, the only friend I've got, asked me how I got the black eye.
"Fell off my bike." I said. It was too late to say anything now. I'd
told a rotten sneaky lie and felt awful about it. But I hate to admit
when someone asks me.

<u>Friday 17th September</u>

Day after day I'm feeling lonelier and lonelier. The only friend
I've got is Mark, and of course, my parents. My other classmates
seem to be on the bullies' side.

<u>Monday 20th September</u>

Oh, no! Conkering season! I can guess what that means.
Boy, was I right. Conkers rained off my head. Seventh years
again. It happens every year. Last year, I had lumps on my head
for a week.

<u>Friday 24th September</u>

I'm feeling upset about the fact I've hardly got any friends, how
people gang up on me and follow me. Why can't I lead a life like
everyone else? What's so different about me?
People having a knock-about with a football. I briefly approach
them. They tell me to get lost. I now feel twice as bad at the
thought of seeing Mark with them. I don't think he knows how

much I feel for him. I don't think he'll ever know. I feel a great deal about my best friend, my only friend.

Tuesday 28th September

I went to see Mr Clay three times today. At last, he's starting to see my problem. I've finally got through to him. He knows what's wrong with me, especially now mum is ringing him.

Friday 1st October

I think I will take up running as a hobby. I'll be able to get away from my enemies, run faster than them. Humph! There's Mr Clay watching me like a hawk, standing all alone in the middle of the playground with my hands in my pockets, feeling sorry for myself. He's been watching me since mum rang him on Tuesday. It's still no good, he never seems to witness me getting bullied.

Monday 4th October

Tripped up in the playground today and banged my knee. That's all I had to do to make three seventh years come over and start laughing at me. One of them pushed me back over. They teased me just because I fell over. I looked across the playground. Was Mr Clay there? Of course not! Why should he be? After all, I'm only getting picked on by three giants.

Monday 11th October

It's almost a week before my birthday. Not that I'm going to get much. It's just something to look forward to.

I think Mr Clay must have something going for Mrs Evans. He's been hanging around with her and chatting to her for the last week. She's definitely been smiling to him when she sees him. That must be something because she's usually an old grouch.

Thursday 14th October

I'm ashamed of Mark. He's told everyone about my birthday, especially the seventh years and I can now guess what's going to happen.

Friday 15th October

I've just had ten bumps to celebrate my birthday. Boy! Am I sore! Up, down; up, down; kicking my backside each time; banging it off the floor. Oh, no! Here they come with the eggs and flour.

Tuesday 19th October

Apart from the ordeal on Friday, I had a good birthday. Oh, dear! Here comes Mr Clay. He must have been told about Friday. Took me to his office and sat me down. "Ouch!"

Humph! He's lecturing on again about this, that and the other. I'm getting tired of this everyday. Why can't he just get round to the point?

Thursday 21st October

I still can't believe it. Mark is my true friend after all. It was him that told Mr Clay when I got the bumps, the egg and the flour. My best friend, Mark.

Friday 22nd October

We're breaking up for half-term. I'll get a rest from those awful seventh years. They'll probably gang up on me today so I shall stay in at dinner time and help clear up the tables. They ganged up on me before last summer. Took me a week to recover. A week off my holiday. But thank goodness last year's seventh years have left now.

Monday 1st November

Back to school again today after one very short week. Back with my best friend,Mark and my favourite teacher Mrs Giles. Today is a quiet day, a mild but wet day. Today's an ordinary day in which the birds sing and the wind whispers in the trees. Today's a very ordinary day in which I'm going to get bullied.

RICHARD'S DIARY (THE BULLY)

Tuesday 7th September 1984

Back to school today. How boring. The only thing I missed in the holiday was beating up that weed, Nicholas. What a wimp! I only have to tap him and he goes to tell the headmaster, Mr Clay, after falling on the floor squawling like a baby.

Wednesday 8th September

Deep inside, I feel sorry for him. My mates and I go round every day and bully him when we pass him. Out comes Mr Clay and gives us a long lecture.

Friday 10th September

Prod! Poke! Slap! Thump! I can't help it; I laugh afterwards together with my mates while all the time I'm feeling depressed. My mum's in hospital. She's been suffering from kidney failure since January. The surgeons can't get more kidneys to replace her infected ones.

Monday 13th September

To make matters worse, my dad's been taking it out on me and beating me. That's probably the reason why I'm bullying Nicholas. I have been since mum went into hospital. He doesn't realize what a stressful time I've been through.

Tuesday 14th September

Oh, dear! Here he comes again.

I laid four on him; I couldn't stop myself. That's probably what my dad thinks when he's hit me.

Wednesday 15th September

Can't find him anywhere today. He must be off, sick. There's no one to take my depression out on. This is probably a good thing. One of these days, I might hurt him seriously then I would be in trouble. The problem is, I'm getting pleasure out of it, especially when I'm with my mates: John; Peter, John's best mate; Paul, my best mate; and Robert.

Friday 17th September

There he is, walking alone with his hands in his pockets.

Why didn't I leave him alone? My mates and I gathered in single file and followed him. He realized what was happening, turned round and shouted "PUSH OFF!" Instead of hitting him, we fell about laughing.

Monday 20th September

Conkering season starts today. Poor Nick! Out came the conkers and rapped him on the head. In he ran, dazed; crying. Out came Mr Clay ranting and raving.

Thursday 23rd September

That Mark must be as big a wimp as Nicholas hanging around with him at times. There they are now. It's strange, the fact we bully Nicholas and not Mark. It's probably because Mark's not as soft.

Mark's just walked away; Nick's a loner once more and there are my mates starting to gather round him.

Tuesday 28th September

My mates have just kicked a football at him. He turned round and it hit him right in the mouth. He's gone in now, he went in with a bleeding lip. Oh, no! Out comes Mr Clay yet again! It's the third time today.

He made me stand, facing the wall with my hands on my head. Why me? My mates have got away with it yet again.

Tuesday 5th October

I'm getting more depressed every day. My father's putting pressure on me and I'm taking it all out on Nick. He was running towards the school this morning and I tripped him up. He fell down and cut his arm severely. At the time that happened, I laughed, but now I feel awful at the thought of it. People must think I'm nasty but it's not my fault. I just can't help myself.

Friday 8th October

There he goes again, limping towards Mr Clay and holding his leg. My mates have just given him more stick. It's alright for them. They get the pleasure out of it while I just take everything out on him because I fell hurt.

Thursday 14th October

Mark has just told us that it's Nick's birthday on Saturday - we had to force it out of him, though. We'll have to celebrate tomorrow instead, bring the egg and flour, give him the kicks and do other things like that.

Friday 15th October

We've just given him ten bumps and pelted him with the eggs and flour. He's now running off home. My mates are still following him, throwing eggs. I've just recovered from laughing, watching them run in the distance with Nick covered in gunge. It's the first time I've laughed like this in ages.

Monday 18th October

Mark's just gone to tell Mr Clay. What a sneak. It must be about Friday. Wait till I get my hands on him. Crumbs! Out comes Mark now, tugging Mr Clay by the hand. Time to hide. He's just caught John and now he's after Paul.

Friday 22nd October

We're breaking up today for half-term and I can't find Nicholas anywhere. I feel so mad. My dad strapped me this morning for not cleaning my teeth. I just want to take it out on him; clear it from my system. He's no where to be seen. I want to make the most of bullying him anyway because I won't see him for a week.

Monday 1st November

Well, it's back to the old school again. What a life. From today onwards, I'm going to cut down bullying Nicholas. When I'm mad now, I'll just count to ten and take my problems out on Mr Clay. He'll understand. He will know why I've been bullying Nick.

Friday 5th November

I didn't tell him until today but he understood and forgave me. I'm a lot happier now. My dad's being looked after by a special hospital and I've gone to a childrens' home for a few weeks until my dad gets better.

Mr Clay is treating me to Himley bonfire tonight. From today onwards, I start a new life.

Appendix 4.2 – Themes in Advertising

The students can use this exercise to debate and consider whether the use of children in the media could be contributing to the problem of child sexual abuse.

How do the images of children and young people in the media affect attitudes towards sexuality and sexual abuse?

What are the advertisers trying to achieve by portraying children and young people as sexual objects?

Have the students collect 'good' and 'bad' examples of images of children and young people used in advertising. These can come from television, newspapers, advertising boards and magazines. Ask them to analyse:

- What the advertiser is trying to sell

- What the overt messages are

- What the hidden messages are

- If they feel the image is 'healthy' and not harmful

- If they feel that this image is harmful and could contribute to the problem of child sexual abuse and why

- If there is anything that can be done about the images that are deemed to be inappropriate

Have the students present their findings either in groups or individually. If they wish, have the class write a letter to an advertiser setting out their concerns.

This exercise can be used as a debate, a research project or a project which could be presented to other classes or to a group of teachers or parents. The students may wish to make a poster or mural using these images and ask other students or teachers for their opinions.

Resources

These resources are listed according to subject matter to give you additional material for follow-up lessons. You will find some materials listed in more than one category because they are useful in different lessons.

Trusting Intuition/ Saying 'No'/Feeling Safe/Safety When Out

Adams, C., Fay, J. and Loreen-Martin, J.
No Is Not Enough (12 years and up)
Impact, 0–915166–35–6
Practical advice for teenagers, and their parents, to enable them to cope with potential assault situations. The emphasis is on prevention and common sense suggestions.

Benedict, Helen
Safe, Strong and Streetwise (14 years and up)
Lightning, 0–340–48495–0
This US book has been adapted for the UK. It contains a massive amount of information and will be especially useful as a reference for schools and parents, as well as for teens themselves.

Elliott, Michele
Keeping Safe: A Practical Guide to Talking With Children (14 years and up)
Hodder & Stoughton, 0–450–43117–7
Straightforward, step-by-step guide known for its low-key and non-sensational approach to children's safety. Based upon common sense and practical techniques, it helps adults to enable children to develop strategies to deal with potentially dangerous situations, from answering upsetting phone calls and coping with bullies, to preventing sexual abuse. The only book of its kind written in the UK, it has been widely endorsed.

Stones, Rosemary
Too Close Encounters and What To Do About Them (12 years and up)
Piccadilly Press, 0–946826–69–2
Based upon common sense and practical strategies for dealing with everything from flashers and rape, this guide is full of valuable ideas for young people. It includes a good resource list at the end for obtaining further help and information.

Flerchinger, B.J. and Fay, J.J.
Top Secret: A Discussion Guide
Network Publications, 0–941816–20–6
Brightly designed guide for teens which goes into rape by
strangers, offenders, acquaintance rape, incest and what to do if
you are sexually assaulted.

Videos

The Suzy Lamplugh Trust
Avoiding Danger, Agreesion in the Workplace
In July 1986 estate agent Suzy Lamplugh disappeared. This
video is an attempt to prevent such a thing happening again by
increasing awareness among both employers and staff of the
potential danger from attack in the workplace.

Bullying

Besag, Valerie E.
Bullies and Victims in Schools
Open University Press, 0–335–09542–9
Without doubt the best book available on the subject of bullying.
The author spent four years compiling research and developing
ways of dealing with the problem of bullying in a practical
manner. A valuable resource for anyone who works with children.

Elliott, Michele
Keeping Safe: A Practical Guide to Talking With Children
See previous section.

Roland, Erling and Munthe, Elaine (editors)
Bullying, An International Perspective
David Fulton Publishers, 1–85346–115–6
This book gives an overview of research and approaches to
dealing with bullying. There are some particularly good
contributions from people like Valerie Besag and Mona O'Moore.

Tattum, Delwyn and Lane, David (editors)
Bullying in Schools
Trentham Books, 0–780948–080227
There are one or two good chapters in this book.

Books for Teens

Cormier, R.
Beyond the Chocolate War
Lion Books

Elliott, Michele
The Willow Street Kids
For teenagers with a 10 to 11-year-old reading level.

Golding, W.
Lord of the Flies
Faber and Faber

Hines, B.
Kestrel for a Knave
Penguin

Hinton, S.E.
Buddy
Penguin

Hinton, S.E.
That was Then, This is Now
Lions Books

Hughes, T.
Tom Brown's Schooldays
Macmillan

Lee, H.
To Kill A Mocking Bird
Heinemann

Maddock, R.
Dragon in the Garden
Macmillan

Needle, J.
My Mate Shofig
Collins

Needle, J.
A Sense of Shame and Other Stories
Lions Books

Swindells, R.
Brother in the Land
Puffin Books

Taylor, M.
Roll of Thunder, Hear My Cry
Gollancz

Waterhouse, K.
There is a Happy Land
Longman

Dramascripts

Calcutt, D.
The Terrible Fate of Humpty Dumpty
Macmillan Education

Casdagli, P.
Only Playing, Miss
Neti-Neti Theatre Company, London

**Crime/Rights/
Responsibilities**

Rae, Maggie
Children and The Law (12 years and up/adults)
Longman, 0–582–89334–8
Clearly explains to young people what their rights are under the

law. Because of the way it is presented, it is also a valuable guide for anyone dealing with young people.

Schneider, Myra
Will the Real Pete Roberts Stand Up (11+ years)
Heinemann, 0–434–95832–8
Put in a children's home when his mother couldn't cope, Pete feels responsible for both her and for the mess at home. His girlfriend helps to set him on the right road, but not before Pete is tempted into petty crime which ends in a terrifying experience.

Rudinger, E.
Children, Parents and the Law (14 years and up/adults)
Consumers' Association, 0–340–37256–7
Very useful and practical book for anyone dealing with questions about the rights of parents and children in legal situations. It is clear, concise and lists many referral agencies for further information.

Ashley, Bernard
Terry on the Fence (12+ years)
OUP, 0–192–71537–2
Terry runs away from home when his older sister teases him beyond endurance. He falls into the hands of a gang from the wrong wide of the tracks, who force him to act as a guide on a thieving raid on his own school. Relationship between two boys from different backgrounds.

Relationships

McCoy, Kathleen
Coping With Teenager Depression (Adults)
Plume, 0–452–25791–3
Written for parents, this practical book is useful for anyone working with teens. Discusses how depression is triggered, how to cope in a crisis such as suicide attempts; also suggestions about dealing with eating disorders, running away, truancy.

Krementz, Jill
How It Feels When a Parent Dies (12+ years)
Alfred A Knopf, 0–394–51911–6
Stories told by children in their own words about the deaths of their parents. Photographs of the children make this a very personal account of dealing with grief. Could be helpful for children trying to cope with bereavement.

Satir, V.
Peoplemaking (adults)
Science & Behaviour Books, 0–8314–0013–5
The author presents her concepts about self-worth, communication, and the family in the form of case histories, anecdotes and a series of communication games.

Rayner, Claire
Growing Pains and How to Avoid Them (12+ years)

Heinemann, 0–434–980420 (Now out of print)

Myles, Gale, Szirom, Davison, Dyson
Taught not Caught: Strategies for Sex Education
LDA, 0–905–114–159
Contains creative and innovative ideas about talking with young people about sexual decision-making and relationships. Includes techniques and activities for working with groups.

Giovacchini, Peter
The Urge to Die
Penguin, 0–14–00–6314–5
An expert in the field of dealing with adolescents and their problems, the author offers practical and reassuring advice about recognising potentially suicidal behaviour and communicating with teenagers in need of help.

Newman, Cathy
Young Runaways
Children's Society, 0–907–32451–7
This report from the Children's Society estimates that 100,000 young people go missing every year and are at risk from prostitution, drugs, petty crime and living in squalor.

Jewett, Claudia
Helping Children Cope with Separation and Loss (Adults)
The Harvard Common Press. 0–916782–53–0
Practical methods and specific techniques for helping children cope with death, divorce, moving, hospitalisation or difficulties with friendships. Useful in therapeutic settings or in schools.

Brenner, Avis
Helping Children Cope with Stress (Adults)
Lexington Books, 0–669–08995–8
Provides guidance for helping children deal with the pressures of divorce, death, illness, and physical, emotional and sexual abuse. Cites specific coping strategies which children develop in each situation and distinguishes healthy strategies from self-destructive ones.

Meredith, Susan
Growing up: adolescence, body changes and sex (11 years and up)
Usborne, 0–860–20837–0
Gives reassuring answers to many questions; packed with information and cartoon-style drawings.

Bawden, Nina
The Runaway Summer
Puffin, 0–140–30539–4
Story of a young girl whose parents are getting divorced and who is left for the summer with her grandfather and aunt. Also involves an illegal immigrant and a policeman's son.

Blume, Judy
It's Not The End of The World
Piccolo, 0–330–25689–0

The story of Karen's feelings watching her parents' marriage fall apart. Sensitively done, American setting.

Bawden, Nina
Squib
Puffin, 0–140–30581–5
A 12-year-old girl whose younger brother was drowned some years ago imagines that a mysterious boy in the park is her revived brother.

Bawden, Nina
The Finding
Puffin, 0–140–32023–7
An exciting story centred around an adopted child's feelings of family ties towards his parents set against his curiosity about his natural ones.

Little, Jean
Mama's Going To Buy You A Mockingbird
Puffin, 0–140–31737–6
Rather a lot worked into this novel, the central premise of which is that Jeremy's father is terminally ill. Jeremy has to cope with all that this entails. Though criticised for the transformation from twelve-year-old to substitute father to the family, and for being over-emotive, this is a book that children will find they can relate to.

Smith, Doris Buchan
A Taste of Blackberries
Heinemann, 0–434–93015–6
A young boy faces death for the first time when he loses his best friend in a sudden tragedy.

Krementz, Jill
How It Feels To Be Adopted
Gollancz, 0–575–03425–4
Interviews and photographs relating to the feelings of nineteen young people coming to terms with adoption.

Krementz, Jill
How It Feels When Parents Divorce
Gollancz, 0–575–03708–3
Nineteen children from the ages of seven to sixteen are interviewed and photographed. American in origin.

Mitchell, Ann K.
When Parents Split Up: Divorce Explained to Young People
Chambers, 0–550–75214–5
Looks at why break-ups can happen, access, divorce law and who can help.

Ashley, Bernard
The Trouble with Donovan Croft
Puffin, 0–140–30974–8/OUP, 0–192–77101–9
Donovan, a ten-year-old Jamaican boy fostered by Keith's parents, is so unhappy that he is unable to speak. Even his own

father cannot get through to him, and it is only Keith's friendship that finally breaks down the boy's wall of silence.

Doherty, Berlie
How Green You Are!
Armada, 0–006–72210–5
Each chapter is a story, but they all feature one set of children from one street. There are encounters with relations, neighbours, friends and enemies in this book about relationships and feelings.

Sachs, Marilyn
The Fat Girl
OUP, 0–192–71534–8
The fat girl is obsessed with Jeff, handsome, popular and 'attached'. He gradually notices her, is at first revolted, but helps her become an individual. Only then do we see what his problems are, as he begins to grow up. Complex but excellent story.

Townsend, John Rowe
Cloudy-bright
Puffin, 0–140–31627–2
The relationship between an insufferable adolescent and an ordinary but nicer girl, and how it develops.

Carter, Peter
Under Goliath
Puffin, 0–140–31132–7/OUP 0–192–71405–8
It is 1969; two thirteen-year-old boys are growing up in the same area of Belfast. One is Catholic, the other a Protestant. Neither really cares about the differences of religion, they are only aware of the common interests of youth. Their friendship is described against the background of public events in Belfast: Orange marches, barricades and bombs.

Video

The Samaritans
Time To Talk (20 minutes)
Designed to help young people to be better equipped to face and cope with crises and to show them how to find someone who has time to talk. Very good, as we have come to expect from the Samaritans.

Abuse/Keeping Safe from Abuse/ Getting Help/ Common Sense Defence

See books listed under the section entitled 'Trusting Intuition' etc., plus the following:

Page, Kathy
Back in the First Person (12+ years and up)
Virago, 0–86068–642–6
The rape of Cath by her former boyfriend leads to a painful year of self-examination and the traumas of going to court.

Eventually Cath moves back into control of her own life. Helpful to young people who have been raped and to others to understand the far-reaching consequences of this kind of violence.

Hart, T.
Don't Tell Your Mother (12+ years and up)
Quartet Books, 0–7043–33772–4
The behaviour and emotions of Shirley and her parents are looked at in depth in this novel about incest. The ending illustrates how the attitudes of society can destroy rather than help. Can be upsetting, but especially useful for exploring the issues with young people.

Moggach, D.
Porky (12+ years and up)
Penguin Books, 0–14–006943–7
A story of incest between father and daughter told with great compassion. Can be used with teens, but should be read by an adult before doing so.

Riley, Joan
The Unbelonging (12+ years and up)
The Women's Press Fiction, 0–7043–3959–5
Eleven-year-old Hyacinth is brought to Britain from Jamaica by her father, a man she does not know. She is hated by her stepmother and beaten and abused by her father. Written with such sensitivity that you want to jump into the book and rescue the child.

Park, Angela
Child Abuse (11 years and up)
Franklin Watts, 0–86313–778–4
Part of a series called Understanding Social Issues aimed at young people, this book looks at issues such as definitions of child abuse, the abuser, the victim and prevention. A help section is also included.

Dahl, Roald
Boy (11 years and up)
Penguin, 0–14–008917–9
Into his description of a wonderful childhood spent in Wales and Norway, the author weaves the story of the cruel and barbaric treatment he received at an English public school. Compulsive reading, as you would expect from Roald Dahl.

Hyde, Margaret O.
Cry Softly! The Story of Child Abuse (11 years and up)
The Westminster Press, 0–664–32666–8
Should be read before being given to young people, but can be a useful tool in explaining to them about how children were once considered property and how many were killed, neglected and maimed. The contact numbers are all US-based.

Chick, Sandra
Push Me, Pull Me (12 years and up)
Women's Press 'Livewire', 0–7043–4901–9
14-year-old girl's world collapses when her mum's boyfriend moves in and sexually abuses her. She tells when he leaves, and the process of healing starts. Winner of The Other Award 1987.

Kempe, C.H. and Helfer, R.E.
The Battered Child (Adults)
University of Chicago Press, 0–226–43029–1
The most comprehensive single volume available on the subject of battered children, it is easily understood, full of essential facts and documentation and contains important new developments in the field.

Kempe, R.S. and Kempe, C.H.
Child Abuse: The Developing Child (Adults)
Fontana Press, 0–00–686120–2
Clearly written and comprehensive guide to understanding child abuse. Written by the acknowledged experts in the field, this book is essential for any library on child abuse.

Kempe, R.S. and Kempe, C.H.
The Common Secret: Sexual Abuse of Children (Adults)
Freeman, 0–7167–1625–9
From the respected pioneers in the field of child abuse, this practical, comprehensive resource gives an insightful look into child sexual abuse, from paedoplilia and exhibition to rape and child pornography. The Kempes allay many of the myths which have hindered a fair appraisal of the problem's severity during the past twenty-five years. Includes details of the Incest Diversion Programme for incestuous fathers.

Wyre, Ray
Women, Men and Rape (Adults)
Perry Publications, 0–870136–00–4
Written in straightforward language, this book is a brief guide to the characteristics of men who rape, with suggestions for potential women victims. It does not tell women what to do, but argues that it might be possible to change the outcome of an attempted rape by understanding more about the rapists. It also identifies potential reforms in the treatment of sex offenders.

Turner, Janine
A Crying Game: The Diary of a Battered Wife (Adults)
Mainstream Publishing, 0–906391–52–0
The author uses her diary of everyday events to describe in vivid detail how she became a battered wife and how she regained her self-respect and helped others. Very useful for anyone who wonders how this kind of violence happens.

Lorrimer, Claire
House of Tomorrow (Adults)
Corgi Books, 0–552–13372–4

Jeanette Roberts, district nurse, has been a foster mother to over 30 children, many so badly abused and ill-treated that they were uncontrollable until she took them into her 'Family'. She was herself abused as a child and has a commitment which is astounding. She is available 24 hours a day to her children and has given them new lives and hope for the future. We need thousands like her.

Camden, E.
If He Comes Back He's Mine (Adults)
Women's Press, 0–88961–090–8
A true story told by a woman who abused her child. Without excuses or self-pity, she describes her own difficult childhood and the pain she inflicted on her son, as well as her relationship with her second never-battered child.

Angelou, M.
I Know Why The Caged Bird Sings (Adults)
Virago, 0–86068–511–X
In this first volume of her autobiography, the author tells about her childhood in the American South of the 1930s. A visit to her mother ends with young Maya being raped by her mother's lover. Through her own inner strength, Maya overcomes this horrific event and goes on to discover the pleasures of dance and drama, and gives birth to a much-loved son.

Bass, E. and Thornton, L.
I Never Told Anyone (Adults)
Harper Colophon Books, 0–06–091050–X
Very moving collection of personal accounts of child sexual abuse written by women of all ages about the abuse they suffered as young girls or teenagers. Introduced by brief biographies that place each woman in a past and present context, the stories reflect a wide diversity of experience and emotional response.

Video

Educational Media International
To A Safer Place (Adults)
The true story of one woman's journey into her past to confront her emotions about the abuse she suffered. One of the best documentaries available about incest.

Addiction/Gambling

Health Education Authority
Smoking and Me: A Teacher's Guide
0–903652–18–8
Materials for use in peer-led smoking education by twelve and thirteen-year-olds. Children select group leaders and under teacher supervision hold group discussions, roleplay and other group-based activities using the five lesson outlines provided.

The booklet also provides background information on children and smoking, fact sheets, useful addresses, a reading list and 7 black and white illustrations which can be photocopied and used as posters.

TACADE/Health Education Authority
Alcohol Education Syllabus, 11–16
A pack consisting of an introductory booklet, plus five individual units, each containing teachers' notes and support pupil material. Written for use with eleven to sixteen-year-olds. 'Year 1' (as the first unit is called) looks at alcohol in society, the history of alcohol use, the effects of alcohol, different types of drinks, and varying attitudes towards alcohol. 'Year 2' explores the drinker as portrayed in advertisements, being under pressure from one's friends, and personal plans of action. The film/video 'In the Middle' can be used in conjunction with this part of the pack. Comprehensive and carefully thought-out material

Department of Health and Social Security/Central Office of Information
Double Take
CFL Vision/ISDD/TACADE
An integrated package consisting of an introductory leaflet, video cassette containing two programmes, teachers' notes and pupil material in support of each programme and a resources guide. One free copy of the package is available to each secondary school in England and Wales from CFL Vision. A comprehensive and authoritative package of drug education materials in two parts for use with twelve to fifteen-year-olds.

The National Housing and Town Planning Council
'The Use of Amusement Arcades and Gambling Machines' (Report)

Carnes, Patrick
Out of the Shadows
CompCare Publications, 0-89638-086-6
Explains the problem of sexual addition which affects people in all walks of life. Not aimed specifically at the sexual abuse of children, but at how people become trapped into using sex as a psychological narcotic which helps them to find relief from feelings of agitation and worthlessness.

Stockley, D.
Drug Warning
Macdonald, 0-356-12424-X
An illustrated guide designed especially to help parents and teachers recognise the various kinds of drugs, as well as the signs and symptoms of drug abuse.

Leaflets

TACADE
Alcohol: Basic Facts

Drugs: Basic Facts
Smoking: Basic Facts
Simple, factual leaflets written for young people. Could be used as basic background information for project work.

Videos

Cancer Research Campaign
Seven Ages of Moron
Yellowhammer Co. Ltd.
In this video, Mel Smith and Griff Rhys-Jones make a humorous attempt to encourage teenagers to see the absurdity of becoming a tobacco addict (i.e. a moron as opposed to a non-smoker). Underneath the banter, serious points are being made about the risks to health, the anti-social side of smoking, how and why not to start, and how to give up if you do smoke.

Health Education Council
In The Middle
Concord Films Council Ltd./CFL Vision
One of a series of trigger films designed to stimulate discussion about alcohol-related issues. 14-year-old Kanay invites some friends round to his house. When one boy starts to light a cigarette and another boy produces some cans of beer, Kanay is caught 'in the middle', torn between the wishes of his parents and the demands of his peers.